In this country it is essential to be dressed for warmth and comfort, for self respect, and for participation in the normal social side of ordinary living. Unless one is so ill that one has to stay in bed, one gets dressed and undressed everyday — no matter what one's disability*, no matter how heavy and helpless one may be, no matter how much it may hurt to put one's clothing on and off. Even the sick person in bed has nightwear regularly changed. Dressing and undressing are normal and obligatory parts of everybody's life, in sickness and in health; and the limitations imposed on opportunity in life are enormous for a person who cannot either dress himself or be easily dressed by others. Dressing and undressing therefore are most important parts of self care for the individual who can manage them independently. For those who cannot, they are an important part of patient care for the nurse, whether she herself is dressing and undressing the disabled person, or teaching family, friends, or other helpers, such as home helps unskilled in this field.

In spite of its practical significance in life, until recently dressing has been a very little considered matter. The Disabled Living Foundation has been working since 1963 on the problems of clothing and dressing, trying to get together an information resource on the subject, both for professional people and for the public. In particular, enquiries showed that there was very little training material concerning dressing available for students or qualified staff in nursing, whether for the various Registers or the Roll. Indeed the Librarian of the Royal College of Nursing confirmed that there was almost nothing on the subject in the Rcn Library, and the Professional Nursing Department of the Rcn informed the DLF that it was felt that more guidance for nurses on dressing of patients would be helpful. This book, most generously financed by King Edward's Hospital Fund for London, both in the compilation of the manuscript and in subventing the publication, is an attempt to supply information on dressing in a form helpful to nurses. The Trustees of the Disabled Living Foundation are deeply grateful to the King's Fund.

Of nearly forty publications to date this book has been the most difficult we have ever had to write. Many methods of presenting the material were tried and rejected. The presentation adopted shows ways of putting on and taking off garments with suggestions of the types of disability which might make it appropriate to use the different methods. It is hoped that the content has been made clear and informative. The DLF Trustees would like to thank the author, Mrs Rosemary Ruston SRN SCM HV, very gratefully for completing an exceedingly difficult task. They congratulate her warmly. The Trustees also thank Mrs Brenda Naylor, whose clear line drawings, based both on photographs and on drawings from life, constitute a most important part of the book. The book owes much to the Editor,

Miss Sydney Foott. It has been produced under the general aegis of the Advisory Panel to the DLF Clothing Projects, and has been steered by a Working Group listed on pages 4 & 5. They have spent much time in discussion and made detailed comments and suggestions. The DLF Trustees much appreciate the help these advisers have given to the author, illustrator and editor.

Dressing disabled people involves nurses in heavy time-consuming work. Being dressed and undressed is often both painful and tiring for such people. All concerned with this book hope that its publication, which is pioneering in its field, will assist in making dressing easier and less distressing for all concerned.

W M Hamilton
Chairman
Disabled Living Foundation

NOTE TO REVISED EDITION

The DLF Trustees are again most grateful to Mrs Rosemary Ruston for scrutinising the first edition of this book, and updating it where necessary. She has done this as a volunteer, and her help has been greatly appreciated. Owing to the sad death of Miss Sydney Foott to whom the first edition owed so much, DLF has a new editor, Mrs Diana de Deney, for the revised edition. The DLF Trustees have been assisted by the King's Fund once more with a generous grant towards this revised edition. They thank the King's Fund most sincerely for the extensive help given over the whole of their work on dressing disabled people, and the more so since the book remains the only one in its field.

W M Hamilton

*It might be useful to quote definitions of words in common use in this field. The word disability or disabled person has been used generically throughout the book unless the other words as below are more appropriate. Disability is the word now used to describe the loss or reduction of ability to do things or, to use a technical term, the loss of functional ability. Handicap describes the disadvantage of having a disability or impairment and the restriction this imposes on a person. Impairment is the actual medical condition of the person. It may or may not respond to treatment (Nichols, P. *Living with a handicap*).

Dressing for Disabled People

ROSEMARY RUSTON SRN SCM HV

Illustrated by
BRENDA NAYLOR

ISBN 0 901908 29 0

First published 1977
Revised 1982
© The Disabled Living Foundation
346 Kensington High Street
London W14 8NS

CONTENTS

ACKNOWLEDGEMENTS

This book owes a great deal to many people—to nurses, occupational therapists and physiotherapists, to the staff of Special Schools, work and rehabilitation centres, and residential units for the disabled and elderly; and to the Aids Centre, Information Service and Clothing Section of the Disabled Living Foundation. Above all, my thanks are due to the many disabled people, and in some cases their relatives, who consented to talk to me in their own homes about dressing and clothing problems, and to the smaller group who modelled so well for the illustrations.

I am indebted to Lady Hamilton, Miss Stow and Dr Monnica Stewart for their constant encouragement, and to the members of my steering committee for their guidance and advice. My especial thanks are due to Miss Sydney Foott for her patience as editor, to Mrs Brenda Naylor for the excellent illustrations and to Mrs Bunce for all her typing and retyping.

R R

MEMBERS OF CLOTHING PANEL (1977)

Chairman
*Lady Hamilton OBE MA
    Chairman of Trustees: Disabled Living Foundation

Members
*Mrs W M Arnett-Rayson SRN RFN
    Nursing/Physical, King's Fund Centre

Miss E Clulow BSc
    Senior Research Officer, Physics Department,
    Shirley Institute, Manchester

*Miss Frances Dean MBE SEN
    Representing the National Association for Mental Health

Dr C M Dorkin MSc PhD
    Leeds University
    Representing the Textile Institute

Miss L Elphick AIMSW
    Social Services Department
    London Borough of Southwark

*Miss M Gilbertson MCSP
    Group Superintendent Physiotherapist
    Hospital for Sick Children, Great Ormond Street

Miss Hubbard
    ILEA — Headmistress, Greenmead School

Miss C King
    Disabled Drivers' Association

Mrs M S T Langton MSc
    Chief Technical Officer
    British Standards Institution, Manchester

Miss P Maccartney MBAOT
    Clinical Tutor, Mary Marlborough Lodge

*Mrs Brenda Naylor
    Dress Designer, Authoress, Lecturer

4

Mrs R Richardson MBAOT
>Information Officer,
>Scottish Information Service for the Disabled, Edinburgh

*Dr M Stewart MB BS D(Obst) RCOG
>Geriatric Unit, Edgware General Hospital

*Miss B Stow MBE FBAOT
>Director, Disabled Living Foundation

Observers
*Miss M Lee SRN RMN
>Royal College of Nursing and
>National Council of Nurses of the United Kingdom

*Dr M Scott Stevenson MB ChB DPE MFCM
>Department of Health & Social Security

*John Tait SRN RMN
>Department of Health & Social Security

Clothing Adviser
*Mrs M Thornton CBE JP MA
>Disabled Living Foundation

*Members of Steering Committee, which also included:
Miss S Foott
>Editor, Disabled Living Foundation

Miss J M Davies SRN SCM HV
>Representative of Health Visitors' Association

Miss C St G Metcalfe SRN
>Representing the General Nursing Council

Sister Clare O'Driscoll SRN ONC RNT
>Representing the Teaching Section, Rcn

CHAPTER 1

THE PROCESS OF DRESSING

Why do we consider clothes to be important? Whether we like it or not, clothes have a bearing on our acceptability by (Western) society. Attitudes these days are not as conservative as formerly: some men and women dress in a very individual manner while others prefer to dress like the rest of their group. A woman usually wants to look different from her neighbour and can wear anything within reason in which she feels happy. A man is more likely to want to dress in the same sort of clothes as the people with whom he associates. Dressing ourselves gives us independence, and clothes express our individuality; however minimal the ability, everyone should be encouraged to dress himself and choose his own clothes.

Dressing (and undressing) is a complex activity; it uses most of the muscles and joints in the body; it requires balance, the understanding of concepts such as inside and outside and top and bottom, co-ordination of hand and eye, the choice of suitable clothes, and knowledge of the correct order in which to put them on. It is scarcely surprising, therefore, that it takes some time for an able child to learn how to dress himself, and dressing may well be affected where disabilities are present or arise later in life. Independence may be gained by adjustment in techniques, choice or adaptation of clothes; for some this may not be possible and they have to be dressed by someone else.

Dressing and clothes are closely related, for example independence in dressing may depend upon having all garments fastened at the front, or made of fabrics which stretch, or sleeves which are raglan rather than set-in; dressing someone else easily may depend on having the minimum of garments, or garments which have back fastenings or which open flat.

Independent dressing for someone of normal intelligence requires one able arm and one finger and thumb able to reach beyond the big toe, or, for those without arms, flexible hips and active toes. Two less able arms or the ability to bend the body or knees may supplement this. Acceptance of a disability (Nichols, P. *Living with a handicap)* leads to an understanding of limitations, and thus to the full use of residual capacities and other assets.

The measure of independence is dependent upon

a personality make up,
b attitude to illness and disability,
c attitude of the doctor and other professional staff to the disabled person and his illness,
d attitude of friends, relations and associates,
e extent of other disabilities, including brain damage, which will require greater resources for adjustment.

Independent dressing for someone of restricted intelligence requires constant repetitive teaching and may never be completely realised. Added impairment or disability may prevent complete independence but does not preclude its partial acquisition, which indeed should be encouraged. (It is important to remember that physical contact by touching is necessary to us all, even if unacknowledged, and being dressed may be the only daily contact a disabled person has. If independence is reached, this contact needs to be provided in another way.)

Dressing has a rehabilitative aspect where:

a it aids the mobilisation of joints and muscles;
b there is a definite and practical aim to which to strive; or
c it shows the doctor, nurse and therapist what movements still need to be taught.

The act of dressing is physiotherapy directed to an essential daily living activity upon which going home may depend. Psychologically, the disabled person gains from being a "complete" person capable of displaying individuality and taste, able to appear socially and ready to receive morale-boosting compliments on his appearance. In rehabilitation, it is important to teach the helper as well as the disabled person so that rehabilitation will continue when he is no longer under the active supervision of the doctor and/or therapist.

Nursing care has traditionally been solely concerned with giving total care to someone who is ill, but increasingly is being supplemented by rehabilitative skills in which the nurse or helper actively encourages independence once total care is no longer required. If rehabilitation is to have real meaning, it should extend beyond specific therapy sessions into normal activity. As the daily activities are normally overseen by nurses or helpers, it is sensible for them to continue using the same rehabilitative techniques throughout the day, to the benefit of the patient, be he disabled, elderly or otherwise unfit. Each person, whether disabled or elderly, is still an individual, and independence gained in some activity where it had previously been lost—a garment chosen or a cardigan put on unaided—can reinforce that individuality. It is easily forgotten that many elderly people are disabled and many disabled people are elderly, so that although not all elderly people require special help or adaptations, many of them could benefit from advice about easier clothing to wear or different ways to put it on. Helpers should know of the skills of other specialists so that they can advise or refer accordingly.

Clothes are important to the human psyche, as can be seen when compulsory removal of clothes can upset mental stability, and uniformity of clothes can impair individuality. The poor condition of clothing or the wrong choice can reduce the worth of the wearer both in another person's eyes and in his own.

So too with the act of dressing; where no expectation is made, no reaction can be forthcoming; unthinkingly dressing someone as if he were a child will encourage the reaction of a child. The expectation of independence in dressing and choice of clothing, in however small a degree, is thus important for someone's wellbeing, whatever his age, aptitude or ability.

Four further important points:

a teaching someone to dress himself may be time-consuming, but once the activity has been learnt both teacher and learner can go on to something new;

b the value of the time and energy spent on dressing oneself needs to be balanced against possible participation in other activities: one disabled person who finds dressing time-consuming and exhausting and who has other interests, by being dressed by someone else can spend his time and energy in employment and more stimulating activities; another without such interests may be stimulated by dressing himself, whatever the time and energy required;

c if normal activity produces fatigue at the end of the day, clothes should be chosen which are easy to remove;

d disabled and elderly people should be expected to choose their own clothes and decide on the best ways to dress or be dressed.

It is hoped that this book will be helpful in dealing with all age groups from the young child to the elderly person. The reader and/or user should therefore keep an open mind towards all the suggestions, whatever the age or sex of the person or people with whom they are working. "He" is equivalent to "she" throughout. "Helper" is intended to include nursing staff, relatives, and all those who help disabled and elderly people to dress and undress themselves.

As undressing is an easier activity, and takes less skill and energy, it precedes dressing in sequence throughout the book. Both are, however, of equal importance.

The book starts by looking at the development of dressing and it is also hoped that this will help those with brain damage who may have forgotten how to dress themselves. Chapter 3 looks at dressing requirements and Chapter 4 at the aspects of clothing for disabled people of all ages. Chapter 5 deals with fastenings and dressing aids in detail, and includes a section on grip and some ways to deal with spasm. Chapter 6 consists of drawings which show the many different ways garments can be removed and put on. These give modifications of both technique and garment where relevant. Chapter 7 looks at some techniques for coping with clothing in the toilet and includes a section on incontinence and the way this affects dressing and clothing. Some conclusions are drawn in Chapter 8 and there are three appendices, on financing and supply of clothing, bibliography and useful addresses.

CHAPTER 2

DEVELOPMENT OF DRESSING SKILLS

There are two major dressing skills: first the physical activity of dressing and secondly an understanding of the characteristics of clothes. The development of these skills is not necessarily related to age.

Dressing

Dressing requires both motor development and co-ordination, capabilities which appear in an orderly, predictable fashion, and follow a definite sequence. Motor development in the young child starts at the head and extends downwards through the arms, hands, trunk and legs, until he can balance on one leg and carry on an activity without falling over. Development of eye-hand co-ordination, in conjunction with the movements of thumb and fingers, change a baby's vague uncoordinated movements into the control and execution of very fine ones.

The ability to start undressing and dressing begins as gross body movements are mastered. Control of the head enables the child to push his head through the neck of vests and jumpers. Control of the arms enables him to push his arms into sleeves and hold out arms for sleeves. Control of the hands enables him to pull socks and slippers off and pull sleeves off. Control of the legs enables him to step out of trousers and pants and hold out his feet for socks and shoes. Control of the fingers enables him to pull a front zip up and down (when the end is held).

Once the gross body movements are mastered the child can move on to more complex activities and movements become finer. Once he can stand up, he balances during dressing by holding on to something or someone else; once able to pull on his clothes by himself, he may prefer to sit down to put on lower half garments until he feels sure enough of his balance to stand on one leg.

Maturity of eye-hand co-ordination and the fine movements of hand and fingers enable the various parts of a garment to be recognised and put on correctly, and for all types of fastening to be mastered.

An order of achievement follows. The order can only be approximate as development differs, but simple activities, once mastered, are always followed by more complex ones.

Motor activities   Arms are put into an open-front garment which is held open. Feet are pushed into slippers. Over the head garments are put on.

Motor activities (cont.)	Pants, trousers and skirts are put on with assistance either with balance or by holding the garment open. Socks are pulled on if the heels are turned out or the socks are loose. Shoes are put on. Caps, mittens and gloves are put on. All garments are taken off when unfastened. All indoor and outdoor garments with simple fastenings are put on under supervision. All indoor and outdoor garments put on without supervision.

Eye-hand co-ordination:

Clothing	Finding the openings of clothes. Placing feet into socks and shoes. Stepping into the correct legs of pants and trousers. Placing hands into gloves or mittens.
Fastenings (Unfastening usually comes first)	Zips (the end from which the tag is being pulled should be held firmly by the helper). Large buttons within reach and sight, especially rounded ones. Toggles. Buckles on belts and shoes. Hooks and bars on trousers and skirts. Press studs. Small buttons, hooks and eyes, shoe buttons. Laces, bows. Open ended zips, back fastenings. Neck ties, top shirt button.

With greater experience much of the eye-hand co-ordination is gradually replaced by "feel". Putting arms into sleeves, adjusting waistbands and doing up many fastenings can be done by "feel" and once this stage has been reached, back fastenings and neckties (with the help of a mirror) can be tackled.

Once dressing skill has been mastered, it becomes a habit, so that more time can be spent on choice, general tidiness, care of clothes and appearance.

The process of dressing involves:

recognition of the different items of clothing;
the order in which clothes are put on;
the way clothes match;

and the concepts of back and front, right and left, top and bottom, and inside and outside.

There are numerous items of clothing, many serving the same purpose. It is helpful if, to start with, clothes are simple, with new kinds of garments being introduced gradually. They can be distinguished by shape, feel, the way they are put on and taken off, and by name, so that eventually a garment can be held up and recognised by looking at it. Colour can be used to differentiate between similar items. (Blind people may be able to use touch.) Talking about the clothes in which a person is being dressed, looking at them in shops or helping to hang them on the washing line all enable him to learn about different garments. If clothes are put on, taken off and laid out in the same order each time, the order is learnt sub-consciously and becomes habitual. Dress sense, or the way clothes and colours match, seems to be instinctive in some people, but much can be learnt by looking at other people's ideas, understanding colour and being prepared to experiment and discovering what clothes suit one best.

The concept of back and front is easiest to grasp in front-opening clothes and fly-front trousers, and most difficult in socks, over-the-head clothes and pull-up pants or trousers. Clothes can be marked to distinguish back and front or use made of a manufacturer's tab. The feeling of discomfort when a garment is reversed may bring understanding more quickly. It may be helpful to lay out clothes front downwards. The concept of right and left depends upon an understanding of oneself in space and relating this to one's clothes, particularly gloves and shoes, but comfort also is involved—soft gloves can be worn on the wrong hands without too much discomfort, leather or rubber gloves cannot; slippers and wellington boots are easier to wear on the wrong feet than walking shoes. Marking clothes, talking about right and left, and looking at the garment and comparing it with the correct hand or foot may be helpful. Buckles on sandals are usually on the outside of the foot. The concept of top and bottom comes with relating clothing with the parts of the body; if arms and head are at the top of the body, sleeves and neck band must also be at the top. Holding up clothes correctly, finding the largest hole, placing garments against oneself, and talking about the concept may be helpful. Understanding the concept of inside and out may be difficult when both sides of a fabric look similar. Linings, the position of fastenings, seams and makers' tabs all give good clues. A knitted fabric is smooth on the outside and rougher on the inside. Taking off the garment without turning it inside out will help. It is easy to put on brassieres inside out, or upside down for those being fastened at waist level; holding the bra up by the straps with the cups facing forward may prevent this.

Independent dressing is a skill learnt over a long period, several years in an able child; disability may delay this or may later demand relearning part of

12

the skill, but it is essential to encourage the skills in dressing so that the desire for independence is encouraged, especially in children.

Teaching dressing skills

The teaching role of a nurse is to do things *with* the patient rather than *to* him. "The patient needs reminding that he can do many things for himself and the nurse should emphasise those things that the patient can do rather that what he cannot. Some will tire easily and will need frequent rest periods. In teaching and helping the patient to learn an activity, he should not be hurried, but should be allowed to work at his own pace. In helping the patient achieve his goal of independence, many problems will develop and extreme patience will be needed by the nurse and all other persons, including the family, who may be working with him (Johnson, D.F. *Total patient care*).

A basic principle of learning is to progress from the simple to the complex, from where the person is to where you both wish him to be. Based on the knowledge of his capabilities, one activity should be taught and mastered before a new one is begun. All improvement, however slight, should be noticed and encouraged. Some people benefit from group work where there is a small element of competition.

The teacher must know what she is doing, why she is doing it, have the skill to carry it out, be able to assess her own progress and should find the work rewarding. A nurse is therefore likely to require assistance and training from therapy staff and others to help her achieve these aims with regard to dressing.

People who have suffered brain damage may have problems such as not knowing where they are in space, or perceptual motor dysfunction (i.e. knows what ought to be done but cannot carry it out). Thus, although they may appear to understand, it is possible that they do not, or they may be able to manage an activity one day but not the next. Dressing is a complex procedure and in these circumstances is best taught after work on increasing concentration and improving the attention span has been done. (This is usually the sphere of the occupational therapist.) An assessment can then be made of any gaps in knowledge and teaching concentrated on these.

The basis for teaching is the same for a learner who has previous knowledge as for one who has not, but for both, the teacher will be better prepared if she is aware of the personality, comprehension, character and willpower of the learner. The teacher needs patience to persevere even when progress appears to be minimal.

1 The amount of ability or residual knowledge of the learner should be assessed.

2 The availability of particular clothing and the techniques of dressing should be known.

3 A programme of teaching should be drawn up, progressing from simple to more complex procedures. Each procedure should be mastered before going on to the next one.

4 The procedure should be demonstrated to the learner and practised as often as is necessary. Constant repetition may be required and it is helpful if the same words can always be used.

5 The pace must be matched to that of the learner.

6 If help is required, a decision should be made whether it is to be given at the beginning, middle or end of a procedure, and if necessary, altered according to progress.

7 All accomplishments, however small, should be praised and capabilities stressed and encouraged.

8 The frustration of those re-learning a habit needs to be understood and ways sought to overcome it.

9 Willingness to try new methods and enthusiasm in involving the learner in these is desirable.

10 The use of a mirror can be of great value. The teacher should stand behind the learner when demonstrating a technique so that the learner learns by seeing and can then copy it himself.

CHAPTER 3

DRESSING REQUIREMENTS

The need for time

Time is an important factor in everyone's life and it can be easy to think that there is not enough time for someone to dress himself. It may seem to be easier and/or less time-consuming to dress him, regardless of ability or potential ability, than to wait and to give help when required. This is not necessarily so, for once that person is able to dress himself more time is available for other things. A look at the way time is used may well be worthwhile.

Does the ward routine demand that all patients be up at a certain time? If so, why? If dressing is considered to be an important part of independence, how much time is in fact spent on it? A number of people requiring help can be put under the care of one nurse, which should reduce the pressure of time. Someone who does not feel hurried may well manage garments not accomplished before. A rigid daily routine, set without due regard to individual needs, tends to institutionalise and does not encourage independence. To be independent in the activities of daily living, including dressing, is part of a person's self respect, and is also often a necessary requirement for discharge from hospital. Time spent in looking at the organisation of the ward as it relates to individual patients and their needs may enrich the lives and work of patients and staff and encourage the learning and use of new skills.

The capabilities of elderly frail people, whether in a home or their own homes, should be regularly assessed. They should be given time to dress themselves if they are able. In this situation ward routine is inappropriate, but they may still be expected to be dressed for breakfast. Is this necessary? If so, is some dressing practice required? Would different clothes or fastenings be easier? (Is financial help required?) District nursing sisters may not be able to give this kind of help or advice during a busy morning's work, but an occasional more leisurely afternoon or weekend visit may be of great value for both the elderly person and any helper. Nursing staff should offer help and guidance in clothing or re-education for dressing to relatives and patients, for they are not always aware that such help exists.

Disabled school children very often have a rigid routine which precludes them from dressing themselves before school starts. There are other times when it is not so difficult—changing after school, at weekends, or during the holidays, when there may be other people around to help or supervise—fathers, other children, staff too busy before school but now available, or voluntary helpers. Independence in dressing is of importance in this group to help them feel more like other children.

The attitude of those caring for disabled or elderly people has a considerable effect upon those they support. Lack of challenge, especially to elderly people, can affect the atmosphere of the ward or home and the morale of all. It is easy for the helper to start helping someone to dress when it is not really necessary. That person may then feel dressing does not matter and give up the activity. A constant interest in his looks and an attempt to attain maximum independence in dressing may have benefits elsewhere, such as bladder and bowel control, and perhaps in greater interest and involvement by neighbours, relatives and friends.

Assessment

The first assessment of dressing abilities should normally be undertaken by therapists, but regular review assessments and long term practice sessions can be performed by those in contact with the disabled person, preferably trained staff, in relevant situations.

Where there are no therapists available, one basis of assessment could be:

a to read the medical history notes, if available, noting any:
   i   basic physical disability,
   ii mental disability,
   iii social history that might shed light on motivation;

b to test for:
   i   comprehension, motivation,
   ii grip,
   iii the amount of shoulder movement,
   iv balance, standing and sitting while dressing, either unaided or with support,
   v   hip movement,
   vi eyesight;

c to ask the disabled person to put on and take off:
   i   a loose garment over the head,
   ii stretchy open front garments with short and long sleeves,
   iii pants or knickers, trousers if appropriate,
   iv slippers and shoes,
   v   tights, stockings or socks as appropriate,
   vi foundation garments if appropriate,
   vii necktie, if appropriate;

d to test the ability to cope with different fastenings:
   i   zips, in front and behind,
   ii buttons—shirt and coat size,
   iii press studs,
   iv laces,

v buckles,
vi Velcro.

At the initial assessment help should not be given unless it is absolutely necessary. The disabled person should, of course, be given an explanation of the procedure. During the assessment, the helper should note where openings and fastenings can be managed most easily, which movements are easiest and least painful, and the amount of energy required. This information should be used to decide on the most suitable clothing, fastenings, dressing aids, adaptations and dressing methods, and a programme of training planned for particular difficulties and special techniques.

How people dress depends largely upon their residual abilities and life habits. The amount of good hand function may well dictate how much dressing can be done. Those with multiple disabilities are likely to do less well than those with a single disability and significant overweight compounds disabilities by increasing the work load of muscles and joints. The energy used in dressing and undressing must be balanced against the amount of energy required for the rest of the day. Being dressed may be preferable for someone who leads a busy active life when dressing himself takes much time and energy. Fatigue at the end of the day should be taken into consideration, choosing clothes that are easy to take off.

Brain damage will affect progress in rehabilitation, and is particularly noticeable following a stroke or other condition where brain function is affected. Severe mental handicap may affect understanding of the process of dressing and the order in which clothes are normally put on. Mental illness may affect comprehension and motivation. The technique of behaviour modification may help to form the habit of dressing correctly, even though the reasons for its success are not understood.*

*Behaviour modification contains a number of useful techniques for teaching people to dress. Courses are held from time to time at The Institute for Mental Subnormality, Wolverhampton Road, Kidderminster, Worcestershire; and the Department of Psychology, Institute of Psychiatry, London University, De Crespigny Park, London SE5.

Some useful references are:

Agras, W.S. *Behaviour Modification.* Boston, Little and Brown, 1978.

Baldwin, V.L. et al. *Isn't it time he outgrew this?* – a training program for parents of retarded children. Springfield, Ill. Charles C. Thomas, 1976.

Karen R.L. & Maxwell S.J. 1967. *Strengthening self-help behaviour in the retarded.* (Amer. Journal of Ment. Def., 1967, New York, vol. 71, pp. 545-550).

Martin, G.L. et al. Operant conditioning in dressing behaviour of severely retarded girls. *Mental Retardation.* Columbus, 1971, vol. 9, pp. 27-31.

Moore, P, and Carr, J. A behaviour modification programme to teach dressing to a severely retarded adolescent. *Nursing Times,* London, 2 September 1976.

Psychological disability may prevent someone perfectly able to dress himself from doing so. The causes of this may be mental illness: for instance depression; over-protection in childhood or acceptance of the dependent role. The importance of encouraging independence in all fields of daily living cannot be overstressed, although it is also important that the motive of the helper is right—the aim of independence is not to save the helper time but to enable the disabled person to achieve greater satisfaction and normal social opportunities.

Assessment should be part of a continuous programme which seeks to improve the progress already made, and should be carried out within a team containing such people as the disabled person, therapists, helpers, the family and medical, nursing and teaching staff.

Rehabilitation

Rehabilitation starts almost as soon as a person becomes newly disabled whatever the cause. It is the aim of rehabilitation to reduce the disability to the minimum and to assist the disabled person to regain basic personal independence in such areas as personal hygiene (including toileting), dressing, eating, mobility, communication and personal safety. Even where this seems unlikely the aim should be kept firmly in mind. Independent dressing and undressing may be affected by permanent disability so that new ways of dressing or different kinds of clothes may have to be devised in order to regain basic independence.

Dressing brings into play most of the muscles of the body, balance, manipulative ability, knowledge of colour and eye-hand co-ordination; and so it can be, and is, used therapeutically. In hospitals medical staff and therapists can assess the ability of the disabled person and plan a programme for him, and nurses should work closely with them to ensure that all are following the same policy. Problems are normally discovered and a programme for the patient planned and carried out either on the ward or in the assessment centre. At an early stage those who are going to care for him should be invited to attend (or should insist on attending) at least one working session, so that his skills and capacities are known to them and the programme continued and assessment maintained.

A training programme should start with undressing as it takes less energy than dressing. When learning or re-learning how to dress, it is best to avoid frustration and fatigue as much as possible, so that the easiest garments and fastenings should be tackled first.

Conditions for dressing

So far as possible, optimum conditions should be provided, including:

1 Time
2 Privacy and warmth
3 Space
4 Garments laid out in order and to hand at an appropriate level
5 Assistance when necessary
6 Suitable furnishings, including good lighting and a mirror
7 Aids to independent movement (wheelchairs, artificial limbs, walking aids, calipers, spinal supports) and dressing aids to hand
8 Willingness to experiment
(The best position in which to dress has already been mentioned.)

1 The right amount of *time* should be available. Someone who is rushed may become confused, give up too easily or need help, when more time might have enabled him to dress himself completely. However, he should not be left too long, as this may mean that he over-tires himself or gives up, or sometimes even reverses the process, taking off garments already donned. Time is also needed to enable him to experiment with new methods or different clothes. Not every disabled person feels able to suggest that another way of doing things may be less painful or faster, so that the helper should ask positively for comment and suggestions.

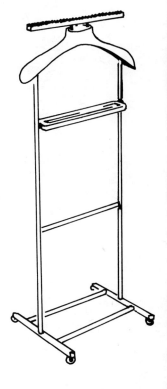

2 *Privacy and warmth* are required for all personal activities such as dressing, but especially for putting on underwear.

3 *Space* gives the helper room to move, and the person dressing room to manoeuvre.

4 Garments laid out *in order* and to hand at the appropriate level. Much time may be saved if garments are laid out in the evening in the order in which they are to be put on the following morning, especially if clean clothes are being provided. They should be laid out on a chair or on a valet stand (commercially available or home made). Shoes should be placed at the level at which they can be reached easily.

5 *Assistance* can be given at any time during dressing or can be limited to seeing that all is ready for dressing to start, or that all is well. It can be given by starting an activity, giving a helpful tug or lift midway, or the finishing touch. How one assists depends upon the personality of the

individual being helped and what he can do. It may be more encouraging to start an activity off and leave him to finish it, or more challenging to leave him to start it and help finish it off if the activity is too tiring or complex for him to complete. In the best interest of rehabilitation, however, assistance should be given only when it is necessary, rather than because it seems such a struggle or it is quicker to do it oneself. Neither of these attitudes is helpful for those who are striving for greater independence.

6 *Suitable furnishings* The floor should have a safe non-slip surface (carpeted or non-slip finish such as cork): a rug could move and is therefore dangerous. If a chair is used for dressing, it should be of a height that enables the person dressing to put both feet flat on the floor, stable, and chosen to suit the person dressing--with arms if support is needed, without arms if it is not.

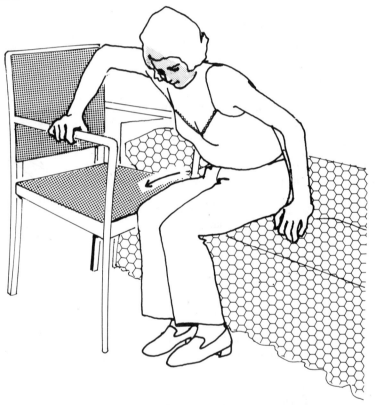

If a bed is used for dressing it should be of a height that enables the person dressing to put both feet flat, at right angle to knees, on the floor when sitting on the side; be at the same height as the chair if the dresser transfers from one to the other; have a firm covering, i.e. coverlet and quilt removed, and have a firm level edge; have enough pillows for support; and be able to support various aids, e.g. rope ladder or pulley if required.

Stable furniture such as a heavy chest of drawers or a locker without wheels can be used as a support while dressing. If temporary support is required, light furniture will be satisfactory if placed against a wall or the wall itself may be enough. A locker or solid chair placed beside the bed can provide support where there is a tendency to fall to one side. A stool or low chair beside the bed for putting on socks or stockings and shoes is helpful. Good lighting is important, especially for the elderly.

A mirror is most important. We all use one, when combing our hair or straightening a jacket, positioning a tie properly or seeing if our colour scheme is right. Yet a full-length mirror is rarely seen in a ward and is not always considered necessary for someone in bed at home. A mirror is a most useful object, for dressing practice, maintaining body image, and for raising morale. It should be at the correct height (see p. 48) and placed in a good light.

7 *Aids,* whether for movement or for dressing, should always be to hand and well supported so that an accidental movement cannot knock them out of reach.

8 *A willingness to experiment* helps both disabled person and helper to keep an open and flexible mind on the best or easiest or least painful way to dress or undress. For instance, if putting on pyjamas is too exhausting at the end of the day, it may be better to sleep in the nude; if bedclothes are too heavy, a continental quilt may be the answer. Men's shoes may be more suitable than the current women's fashions. If an old man has always slept in his vest and pants, a change may be demoralising, so it may be best to allow him to continue in his usual way. It is not always easy to persuade an elderly lady to give up her corsets when she has worn them for years, although the struggle to put them on may now be too much for her; encouraging her to look at other styles, different ways of keeping up her stockings, and even exercise or diet, may help her to change or relinquish the corsets. Being fully dressed is to be aimed at, especially in long stay homes and hospitals, but there may be some circumstances, especially for some younger disabled people, where leg deformity or other disability may be so severe that the easiest garment should be worn.

Similar conditions apply to those who are being dressed by another. The number of people able to do little or nothing for themselves is small, and sufficient time for them to do what they can helps to preserve some independence. Disabled people can be dressed either on the bed or sitting in a chair, and the choice depends on what is easiest for the helper. A common practice is to put on underclothes and trousers (if worn) while the disabled person is lying on the bed, for the pants and trousers to be pulled up during transfer from bed to chair, and for the rest of the clothes to be put on once he is seated on the chair.

The mirror helps to preserve the image of the self which can be lost remarkably easily, and should always be available and used.

Grip or Grasp

The grip or grasp is used to hold on to articles or objects. Small articles are held between the thumb and forefinger and power is exerted over a small area. Larger articles are held in the hand, the fingers curving round the object and the thumb acting as a counterbalance. For various reasons, these two activities may be curtailed or absent. The drawings illustrate alternative ways of holding an object.

Friction, obtained by wetting the skin or rubbing it against a rough surface, can help to improve the grip. Some degree of spasm in the wrist or hand, if it can be controlled, may enhance the grasping power of the hand.

Lifting ability can be increased by supporting the elbows on a firm surface, by using both hands together, or by using an able hand as a lever beneath a passive hand.

Spasm

Spasm is found in many different conditions and can cause pain and delay in carrying out an activity. In the child with cerebral palsy, spasm can counteract any training he may be having to control his abnormal movements; helpers should try to continue the training during dressing practice. Spasm can also be used with grip if it is in the right place and can be summoned at will. Limb spasm can be relieved by rotation, shaking the limb, or compression through a joint. Body spasm can be helped by bending over and breathing deeply. Where spasm is due to sensitivity to touch, stretching a limb before starting an activity may be helpful, on the principle that the more the body is touched, the less sensitive it becomes, resulting in a reduction in spasm. The extension spasm of a palsied child can be relieved by crossing his arms and he can then be bent forward from the hips.

Anti-spasmodic drugs can be given half an hour before activity starts.

Preservation of dressing skills

People who are already disabled may be admitted to hospitals or other institutions or into the care of the district nursing sister for reasons other than their disability. They and their relatives have lived with their particular problems for some time and may well have found satisfactory answers. It is, therefore, sensible for all those staff coming in contact with the disabled person or his caring relatives, to ask how he manages his daily living activities—eating, dressing, walking and so on. Although it is usual for relatives to be asked about these details at the beginning of treatment, it is difficult for every area to be covered in full and so it is advisable that they should, if necessary, be asked to repeat the details on subsequent visits.

It is the duty of the person receiving the information both to ensure that it is passed on to everyone likely to be caring for the disabled person, and to emphasise that the latter must always say how he likes help to be given. Most helpers prefer to know the way in which a disabled person likes to be lifted, dressed, and so on, but if staff change frequently the disabled person himself must be prepared to repeat the information. The person in charge should impress upon staff and other helpers that they should always ask for information, and accept what the disabled person says. To ask is a courtesy, not an expression of ignorance.

Once the disabled person has been receiving care for a time, it may be worthwhile looking at the dressing and undressing procedures, discussing with therapy staff whether there are better methods or different sorts of clothes which would improve his performance or help the people dressing him. Not everyone likes change, so that any alteration should be introduced gradually and tried out as an experiment. The opinions of relatives should also be taken into account and if any changes are made, they should be involved. Being cared for by someone else may bring new light to bear on a method that has been accepted for years as the "only possible way".

Some disabled people have a very frail grip on their independence in dressing and it is important for them to be encouraged to retain it. It may be very easy to dress them because it looks painful or they are rather slow, but the loss of this independence may make an enormous difference to continued acceptability when they return home. Whatever the reason for admission, the person should not be discharged having lost an area of independence, unless the cause of his admission marked a further deterioration of his condition which could not be countered. This is one way in which care staff should have regard for the relatives who will continue looking after the disabled person after his discharge.

If the disabled person is unable to communicate his needs, then it is important that the ways those needs are dealt with are known to everyone, plus the signs or indications made by him that something is wrong. This is a communication problem which must be solved either by having only informed people caring for him or, with the disabled person's permission, by writing everything down near the bed and ensuring that everyone knows it is there and reads it. Such information should not be exposed to casual gaze.

If the disabled person has special clothing, arrangements for laundry and/or replacement need to be considered.

Contact with other disciplines

This is most important. Teamwork is essential because it is not possible for one profession or one person to be the repository of all skills and all knowledge.

1 With regard to dressing and undressing, professional advice should be available from:

Occupational therapists, who are experts in the field of daily living activities which include dressing, and can help in the evaluation of different techniques, clothes, adaptation and aids.

Physiotherapists, who are experts in the field of movement, and can suggest techniques of dressing which use specific muscles and joints, so that two purposes may be served—a dressing technique used as physiotherapy.

Speech therapists, who may be able to help with people who drool and can give advice with communication problems.

Stoma therapists, who can advise on comfort and clothing, the minimisation or elimination of leakage and helpful clothing where necessary.

Therapists are now more easily available to nursing staff for consultation and advice, as the trend is to work with disabled people where they are, in the ward or in the home, rather than in a department (which is the place for more specialised treatment or group activities). However, therapy staff can spend only a limited time with each person, while the helper is there for 24 hours, so that very clear channels of communication need to exist between the two. The treatment started by therapy staff should be continued by helpers and the effects of that treatment should be communicated back. Teamwork of this kind, which should include the disabled person and visiting relatives, is more likely to produce positive results than the situation where there is a lack of such information.

2 With regard to clothing, professional advice should be available from:

a Supplies officers, who order the clothes and need feedback from the users to know whether the clothes are suitable for the purpose. They have access to manufacturers and clothing catalogues and should be able to give information on the qualities of different fabrics.

b Laundry managers, who are responsible for the quality of laundered articles. Sewing room supervisors and tailors who are responsible for repairs and clothing and who may sometimes alter garments.

c Clothing managers, who should be co-ordinators between patients, relatives and nursing staff, and supplies officers, laundry managers, linen room supervisor, etc. It is helpful if they have some knowledge of the properties of textiles.

d Nursing sisters, some of whom have specialised knowledge in this field.

All groups of staff have problems which impinge on the work of other groups but many can either be avoided, answered or at least partially solved by accurately stating what the problem is and bringing together the relevant groups of people concerned, including those from the sewing room. Where a clothing manager is employed, it should be easier for problems to be seen and resolved and for clothing policy to be clear.

Manufacturers are occasionally willing to help with experimental clothing and can make helpful suggestions about making up and design, especially if they feel that a regular contract or large order may result.

Shopkeepers may be willing to stock certain lines, especially if assured that there will be a reasonable demand.

Where clothes are bought in quantity, it is easier administratively for them to be standardised. This may be acceptable for underwear or socks but is much less satisfactory for personalised clothing, especially with regard to shoes and clothing for people who are not stock size. Those who direct buying policy need feedback of information, such as the results of previous policies with regard to comfort, acceptability, durability, launderability and appropriateness, plus details about individual needs, new garments and fabrics. Trials should become normal practice when considering a change in buying policies, so that the right decisions can be taken.

It is possible these days, even with bulk buying, to provide choice of design, fabric, and colour, and to have sufficient variety to clothe a group of disabled people without disabilities being emphasised. To do this, however, requires knowledge of clothing available, flexibility of attitude, discretion in selection, perseverance in obtaining it and watching for results, and knowledge of its maintenance.

Chapter 4

CLOTHING REQUIREMENTS

Clothing for disabled people should be:

1 Fashionable and pleasing
2 Easy to put on
3 Comfortable to wear
4 Durable, especially in areas of heavy wear
5 Easy and satisfactory to wash or clean
6 Safe

1 *Fashionable and pleasing* clothes are as important to disabled people as to any other group. Today's fashions vary enormously in length, fit and style, and should be chosen by disabled people, their friends, helpers, nurses and others with a view to what will best suit them. Each person is different, e.g. an older woman may be less worried about current fashion and more concerned with durability, fit and comfort than a young with-it teenager. Some people would prefer to wear fashionable and off-the-peg garments, even if they need help with dressing, while others may prefer to wear something specially made or adapted, so long as they can dress themselves. Personal preference is most important, and cannot be too highly stressed.

2 Clothes that are *easy to put on* may seem an obvious point, but such clothing must be acceptable. For instance, a man who has always worn a suit and then develops a muscle weakness in his arms may want to continue wearing his suit to work, although the coat is now difficult to put on, or a woman with multiple sclerosis prefers to wear dresses which fasten at the back. If people feel that their self image is being attacked, it is likely to put them on the defensive and to make them obstinate. It is better to help them to dress and try to influence them gradually, especially if a desire to be independent in their dressing can be stimulated, perhaps by finding new garments or techniques of dressing.

Most disabled people find that easy to put on clothes—
are at least one size larger than their real fitting;
are made in fabrics or styles which "give" (have some elasticity);
have the minimum of fastenings, which are easy and in the most accessible places;
have seams which are flat, strongly sewn and do not lie over pressure points;
have good sized openings;
can be slipped on without catching on another garment.

3 *Comfortable to wear* covers a number of factors: warmth, weight, elasticity, texture, absorption and static electricity.

a Warmth. Clothes are warm when they trap an insulating layer or layers of air round the body and thus prevent loss of body heat. This is especially important to those handicapped people whose sensation or mobility is reduced. In still air, the thicker a fabric and the more open its structure the more air it will trap and the warmer it will be. In a wind or draught, the outer layer of clothing needs to be closely woven to prevent air movement and thus loss of heat from the inner layers. If a person has no feeling in his extremities, it is impossible for him to tell whether these are hot or cold, and protection is required.

Warm *fabrics* include: fur, wool, fabrics with a pile, quilted fabrics. Warm *clothes* include: lined clothes, string vests or loosely knitted wool garments if worn underneath a closely woven garment, several layers of lightweight clothes.

Cool *fabrics* include: thin, loosely woven or knitted fabrics which allow plenty of air movement.

Cool *clothes* include string vests, sleeveless garments, loose or "open" style clothes.

Tight clothes or those which are felted or shrunken restrict the circulation and the wearer feels cold. Fur is a warm material, although it can also be bulky.

b Weight. Heavy clothes tend to restrict movement and are difficult to take off and put on. Weight can also cause further pain. Light clothes help maximum movement, and dressing is easier. Disabled people should be encouraged to wear clothing that is both warm and light, made from materials such as single and double jersey, wool or acrylic knitwear (see section on safety), or pile, quilted or brushed fabrics.

c Elasticity reduces strains on seams and allows for greater freedom of movement when dressing or undressing, the garment subsequently regaining its normal shape.

It is found in: i fabrics containing rubber or elastomeric yarns (Helanca, Lycra).

ii fabrics constructed in such a way that stretch is incorporated (knitted fabrics, fabrics made from textured yarns such as bulked nylon or polyester).

iii garments made in such a way to allow stretching (cut on the bias, or incorporating stretch features such as ribbed fabric at waistband or cuffs or stretch fabrics in the tops of socks or stockings).

Elastic contains rubber yarns and usually exerts more pressure on the body than fabrics containing elastomeric yarns. Elastic garters that are too tight will restrict circulation and produce swelling, and although "stay-up" socks and stockings are better these also must not be too tight. Overstretching the "elastic" tops of socks and stockings will reveal the elastic content which may then be cut to relieve the tightness.

d Texture. The fabric can feel pleasant or unpleasant to the wearer. Soft, warm-feeling fabrics give the most pleasant feeling and usually contain a high proportion of natural fibres.

Stiff, unyielding materials, e.g. denim, drill, sailcloth, heavy taffeta or rough tweeds should be avoided by anyone having to sit for long periods, for whom easy care minimum crease fabric is best; knitted fabrics, fine cotton or viscose rayon fabrics or those made from textured synthetic fibres are more flexible. Slippery materials such as satin, some synthetic fabrics and those commonly used as linings and for underskirts enable the body to slide easily from one surface to another, e.g. from a bed to a chair. A debilitated person wearing these fabrics and sitting up in a bed or on a chair will tend to slip. "Hairy" fabrics such as Harris tweed and some other woven woollen materials should be avoided by those with sensitive skin, some skin conditions and allergies, or extensive scar tissue. Wool worn next to the skin can be irritating and may exacerbate exzema in some children, and although this effect is reduced if the article is lined, it is probably better to use alternative materials.

e Absorption. Perspiration is the result of a normal physiological function, varying in amount according to the individual. If the sweat is not completely absorbed by air or clothing it can be both uncomfortable and damaging to the skin, especially for those unable to move as air circulation helps to absorb the moisture.

Absorbent *fibres* include natural fibres, viscose rayon
Absorbent *fabrics* include knitted fabrics and towelling
Fibres with poor absorbency include polyester, polypropylene and some other artificial fibres
Fabrics with poor absorbency include thin woven fabrics; some drip dry and anti-crease fabrics.

Polypropylene can be used as a one-way fabric if it has an absorbent layer of material behind it; moisture will pass through it one way on to the layer beyond it, and the moisture will not return until the absorbent layer is saturated. It is therefore useful for underwear, under plaster heavy braces or corsets, and as sheets and liners for those who are incontinent, as it keeps the skin dry and thus reduces the risk of pressure sores. Polypropylene when hot and in large quantities as in a hospital laundry drier can be a fire risk, so that polyester, which is almost as non-absorbent, is increasingly being used in its place.

Anti-perspirants can help reduce underarm perspiration for men as well as women, and dress shields help to prevent it reaching clothing. It is unwise to use vaginal anti-perspirants, especially when there is a heavy discharge, as this is a problem which should be dealt with by medical advice.

Some of the man-made fibres, including nylon, do not inhibit the development of unpleasant odours on garments even when they are laundered regularly. Cotton is a good fibre for underwear and nightwear where there are special perspiration problems, for example under heavy breasts, or in the groin, especially for chairbound people who cannot move or where insufficient fresh air reaches the area; easy care cotton is easy to launder and absorbs perspiration better than synthetic fibres.

f If static electricity causes discomfort to the wearer, it is advisable either to obtain clothing made from a "mixed" fabric (synthetic + natural) or one which has an anti-static finish, or to buy underwear in the new anti-static nylons. It is also possible to use a fabric softening rinse.

4 The *durability* of a fabric depends on the strength of the fibre and the construction of the fabric. The stronger the fabric, the less pliable it is and therefore the less easy to wear, so that a compromise may have to be made between durability and ease of wear. If strength is required only in certain areas—sleeves for wheelchair users for instance—it is obviously better to reinforce the areas concerned. Lining garments increases their life span, and is especially recommended where there is likely to be excessive wear, where crutches, calipers or spinal supports rub against the clothing, or where one part of the body is constantly moving against another or against a firm object, such as pressure between knees or when propelling a wheelchair. Many hints on the ways clothes can be preserved and repaired are given in P. Macartney's *Clothes sense* pp. 57-60. Toes of shoes can be strengthened by painting on a transparent acrylic film when new, or by fixing toecaps.

Destruction of clothing is a symptom of disturbed behaviour which may become habitual, so that preventing the habit from forming is the best form of management. Distraction, interesting occupation, involving the person in choice of clothing and colour may help to minimise destructiveness. Continuous wholesale destruction of clothing is most easily coped with by using full-length garments made of nylon taffeta or terylene/cotton but constant efforts to enable the person to wear normal clothing should continue to be made. (Nylon taffeta is a hard and shiny fabric, cold to the touch and not very comfortable to wear, while terylene/cotton is softer and warmer to the touch and more comfortable, so is likely to prove more acceptable.) Styles should enable the helper to put the garment on easily, but any fastenings must be out of reach of the wearer. Garments without fastenings such as tunics, casual shirts and elastic waisted trousers give less opportunity for picking, while the absence of constriction may be less irritating to the wearer.

Short sleeves are cool and less accessible.

Underwear should aim at decency if the top garment is destroyed.

Where only particular areas are vulnerable reinforcement gives a wider choice of garments and fabrics.

Knitted fabrics are easy to unravel, particularly the weft-knit structures used in cardigans, so that these should be worn underneath the main garment if extra warmth is required.

Clothes are an expensive item in any budget, and it is a normal reaction to buy a cheaper article if one is available. Cheap clothes may become expensive, however, if a disability puts a strain on an area that is not made to bear it and replacement is necessary. Fashion-conscious people may prefer replacement at a time when fashions change rapidly but those who are cost-conscious will know the importance of durability which may save money in the long term. Much, of course, will depend upon the financial position of the disabled person. Nursing staff, especially health visitors and district nursing sisters, should be prepared to discuss this aspect of clothing (see Appendix I).

When clothes are hand-made, individual features can be incorporated into the design, and if the fabric and the dressmaking are good, the garment should last for a considerable length of time. For a hand-made garment to be durable implies good dressmaking practice and therefore good finishing techniques. Bespoke tailors or multiple tailors making ready made-to-measure suits may be willing for a small charge to incorporate reinforcing panels.

Durable clothes include those suited to the disability; made of suitable material; able to stand continued washing or dry cleaning, and not too fussy in design or too quickly dated;
and those with good seam allowances; firmly sewn fastenings; a full lining where suitable, suitable reinforcement where necessary, and raglan sleeves or well-fitting to the armhole and across the back.

5 *Launderability* is a quality which, with the increasing number of synthetic/natural fabrics and finishes now on the market, is becoming more difficult to describe. It is necessary to know the content of the fabric or to keep the label of the garment in order to know how it is best washed. The HLCC (Home Laundering Consultative Committee) instructions on detergent and washing powder packets are also excellent guides.

There are, however, many difficulties. Laundering is relatively simple if fabrics are known, labels retained and the laundry is under the control of the person who sees the process through from taking off the dirty garment to putting the clean one on again. If a third person is involved, mistakes can be made, for instance articles to be dry cleaned are washed; a woollen shawl goes to the laundry instead of being hand-washed; and nylon nightdresses loose their colour because the temperature of the water is too high. If mistakes of this kind occur in institutions it is important that a laundering policy for each new fabric (before its introduction) is formulated by those concerned e.g. laundry manager, supplies officer, nursing staff. Money is wasted if it is spent on clothing later ruined in the laundry.

Fabrics in common use can be graded in terms of the severity of the washing treatment they will withstand. The further down the list they are the lower the temperature at which they can be washed and/or the more care has to be taken in the subsequent removal of water.

> White cotton or linen without special finishes
> White nylon or polyester/cotton mixtures without special finishes
> Coloured cotton or linen, rayon, without special finishes
> Coloured nylon, polyester/cotton mixtures
> Polyester, acrylic/cotton mixtures
> Cotton and rayon with special finishes
> Acrylics, acetate, triacetate
> Wool, wool blends with other fibres
> Silk

Some synthetic fibres attract dirt and should be washed frequently as they may be difficult to clean if they become very soiled. Static electricity attracts dust, but some manufacturers claim that the attraction can be reduced if fabric softening solutions are added to the final rinsing water.

Drooling is a distressing symptom which can sometimes be helped with exercises from the speech therapist, and in a child will sometimes disappear when full dentition has occurred. Clothing needs to be fully protected, especially on the shoulders and chest, by an apron or bib made of absorbent fabric backed with flexible polythene, which should be changed when wet. If spit does get on to clothing, it tends to leave a white mark after washing which can be removed by brushing and rewashing. Wool and loosely woven fabrics are not suitable in garments near to the head as they tend to matt. Easy-care and durable fabrics are best. Spit also prevents the easy movement of zips so that front zips, for example in anoraks, should be covered. Dresses with interchangeable bibs are pretty and practical. T-shirts and nylon shirts and jumpers are easy to wash and do not matt or shrink. Ties are impracticable for daily wear: a scarf or cravat in the neck of a coat absorbs the spit and keeps it away from other clothes.

6 *Safety*

   a Fire. Some fabrics burn more easily than others, a factor which must always be taken into consideration, especially where smoking is a hazard both for the smoker and for those around him. Children and elderly or confused persons should wear non-flammable materials, especially for night-wear. Anyone not wearing flame resistant fabrics should not approach a fire, either coal, electric or gas, or paraffin heater. This is especially dangerous for those wearing long dresses or nightdresses (pyjamas are much safer). Fires should always be guarded.

Fibres which *flare* include cotton, linen, rayon, cellulose, acrylics, acetate (lightweight fibres flare more readily)

Fibres which *melt* include nylon, polyester, flame resistant acetate (Loflam Dicel)

Fibres which *smoulder* include wool, silk

Flame retardant fibres include Nomex nylon, chlorofibres, modacrylics, flame-retardant rayon (Darelle)

Fabrics which *burn* include heavyweight fabrics in fibres which melt and lightweight fabrics in fibres which smoulder

There are also a number of flame-retardant finishes on the market, but in order to maintain flame-retardancy in both fabrics and finishes, the washing instructions must be strictly followed.

Laundering in soap in hard water areas may lead to a gradual accumulation of lime soaps, which are flammable, and can increase the flammability of fabrics in time. The use of synthetic detergents instead of soap avoids this danger (and suitable detergents are so marked on the packet).

Fibres that melt normally extinguish themselves because the burning molten material falls away. However, if a natural fibre is blended with a fibre that melts, such as cotton/polyester, the natural fibre will support the molten synthetic fibre and prevent it from dropping, and consequently the fabric burns fiercely. In the same way, a cotton garment with a nylon lining may form a highly combustible combination. It has also been found that if a cotton sewing thread is used in a polyester or nylon garment, a flame will run along the length of the stitching. When making a garment of flame retardant fabric therefore, accessories such as thread, lining and trimmings should be of a similar type of flame retardant material.

b   Slipperiness. It is possible for someone to be let fall when being lifted if the clothes are slippery. Two slippery surfaces together are also unsafe, as with nylon clothes on the polished seat of a chair. New leather soles should be roughened, and floors polished with a non-slip polish.

c   Miscellaneous. Some garments can be unsafe in certain circumstances, for example the fringed edge of a poncho can get caught in wheelchairs or in door hinges; the strings and toggles of a windcheater or anorak can become entangled in moving parts. Untied shoelaces can cause tripping. Skirts that are too full can catch in the wheels of wheelchairs, and full skirts or trousers that are too long and baggy can cause the wearer to trip. Articles that are torn or worn may become caught up in handles or other projections and so may be dangerous.

Someone dressed in synthetic fabrics and left in the sun in a restricted space may build up a dangerous body heat which cannot be reduced by the normal mechanism of moisture being evaporated by the movement of cool air. Babies left in cars in the summer are especially vulnerable.

CHAPTER 5

FASTENINGS AND DRESSING AIDS

Fastenings

Correct fastenings in the right place can make independent dressing possible. Careful thought should therefore be given to the type and position of fastenings when choosing a garment, or even the avoidance of fastenings altogether.

The function of fastenings is to close openings.

Neck and shoulder openings

front

side

back

Openings are found at the neck, shoulder, front (complete or halfway), side, back (complete or halfway). Side openings gape less than front openings.

In unaided dressing where it is difficult to bend the elbows, avoid fastenings at the neck; where there is poor sensation, openings and fastenings should be within sight: a mirror can be helpful; when sitting in a chair, long back zips are suitable only where the top half of the body is freely mobile; a wrap-around skirt may be easier for those who remain seated, but means increased bulk in front.

In aided dressing: back-opening clothes are easier to put on, especially for those with stiff or painful shoulders or where the person is lying supine. They are also helpful for wearers who are destructive, confused, pluck at fastenings, undo fastenings or remove clothes.

Fastenings should be: within reach—front and side fastenings are easiest; within the capacity of the disabled person to use; used with aids if they will facilitate independence.

The various types of fastening are described under the following headings: Description/diagram; abilities required for use; advantages and disadvantages; other points.

a *Velcro:* the touch and close fastener.

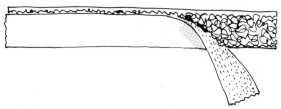

Once put together, the two sides hold fast until they are pulled apart.

Abilities required for use: minimal pressure is required to lock the two strips; some grip to pull them apart, one side being held firm; the two strips need to be lined up accurately.

Advantages: it is easy to use; it can replace many conventional fastenings, e.g. buttons, zips or shoe buckles. It is best used in dabs rather than in long strips—in adaptations this is less expensive, and it is easier to line up. It is not as uncomfortable to lean on as buttons or zips at the back of a dress.

Disadvantages: it must be closed before laundering—lint from other garments gets caught in the hooks side of the Velcro, making it unusable. (It is possible to clean it with a special brush but this takes time.) It makes a "tearing" noise on being opened. Hooks can snag or catch on other clothing, especially stockings or woolly materials.

The hook side of the fastening is abrasive and so should not be in contact with the body.

It can come undone if the garment is too small, or the length of Velcro used is too short, or it becomes matted.

It cannot be fastened down the back by the wearer.

It is not always easy to line up correctly so should not be used on closely fitted garments.

It is available in a variety of colours and widths. Where it is used down the front of garments, sew buttons at regular intervals for appearance.

b *Hooks and eyes, hooks and bars*

There are many sizes; the larger ones are more useful for the handicapped person. The large size tends to be bulky; the rest are flat and neat.

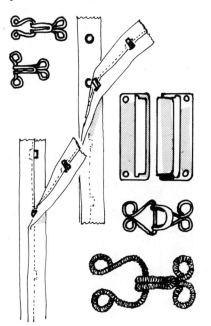

Abilities required for use: the hook needs to be picked up and placed into the eye or bar, which must be held. Larger sizes are easier to use because they are easier to grasp. Exposure of the eye may make it easier to put the hook in.

Advantages: it provides a flat, invisible fastening. The hook and bar is easy to handle on waist-bands unless the garment is on the tight side.

Disadvantages: small hooks and eyes are hard to see, feel and use. Hooks and bars are more difficult for other people to fasten, especially when they are under tension.

Prising the hook apart a little more may make it easier to fasten.

Hooks and eyes are used a great deal in corsetry. One-handed people may find the Kempner fastener (see c) or D/ring easier to use.

Replacing small hooks and eyes with larger ones may be helpful.

Some one-handed people whose trousers or skirts are fastened with a hook and bar may have trouble fastening it if they cannot anchor the bar. Sew a tab on the end of the waistband holding the hook to lengthen it; pull the tab well over the bar, let the tab move back close to the waistband and the hook should catch on to the bar.

c Kempner fastener

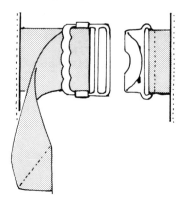

Very suitable for one-handed users.

Abilities required for use: the bar must be stabilised and there must be enough grip to place the hook over the bar and to pull the strap to tighten or loosen it.

Advantages: it can be used one-handed. It enables a garment to be opened out flat. When used on a front-fastening brassiere, it anchors the bottom, so enabling the rest of the fastenings to be done up.

Disadvantages: it is difficult to attach to a short length brassiere—a long-line one is much easier to adapt. (Velcro with a D-ring may be easier for a short length one.)

The pull should be towards the functional hand. The free end of the strap should be stitched back to prevent it from being pulled out of the bar, and this can be used as a loop if the wearer finds the strap difficult to grasp.

d Buttons and buttonholes

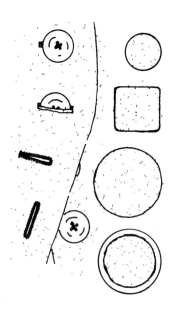

Round buttons which are ball shaped or with a ridge at the edge are easiest to manage.

Abilities required for use: reasonable sight or sensation is required. Grip by the thumb and forefinger of at least one hand; fine movement of thumb and fingers.

Advantages: normally they remain closed unless tension exists in the opposite plane to the buttonholes. They can be a decorative feature. A button can be fastened one-handed; a dressing aid is available for those with poor grip (a buttonhook—see p. 49).
Large, round buttons are easiest, especially for children; the toggle and frog fastening is good on heavy fabrics.

Disadvantages: fine movements are needed.
Small buttons are difficult.
Care must be taken to match type and weight of button to the weight of the fabric.

Buttons raised from the fabric are easier to handle, especially when grasp or co-ordination is poor. They can be raised by sewing on with long shanks, backing the top button with a smaller button, or putting two buttons together as one.
Stretch cuff links can be made by linking two buttons with shirring elastic.
A cuff button sewn on with elastic enables a hand to be pushed through the cuff.

Buttonholes.
They can be bound, worked, be part of the seam, or looped.
They should be well placed to prevent gaping.
Vertical ones are easier to manage than horizontal ones, but are more susceptible to tension.
Bound and worked holes are easy to feel.
Loops are easy to manage.
Buttonholes are weakened by "worrying" with the thumb and forefinger: this is certainly a way of undoing the button, but a buttonhook may be easier.

e *Tapes, laces*

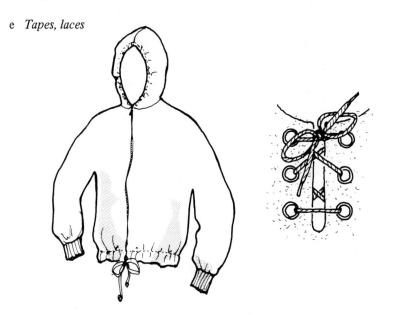

Abilities required for use: the ability to tie a bow and/or knot is required.

Advantages: tying laces or tapes can be done one-handed as long as one end is fixed.
They draw a garment up to fit.

Disadvantages: it is very difficult to do up oneself if the tapes are at the back.
The ends can catch in wheels, doors, etc.
If the tapes are at the back the knot is painful to lie on and can cause pressure sores.
Tapes are easily torn off, especially in the laundry, and difficult to untie when they are wet.
The tapes themselves can easily become knotted.

They can be replaced by elastic.

f *Zips*

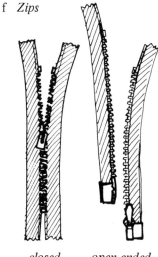

closed   open-ended

The "invisible" zip is lighter in weight, but more difficult to open and close.

Abilities required for use: zips require a grip firm enough to pull the tag up and down. Some method of anchoring the end of the zip being pulled away from is required. Good eye and hand co-ordination is needed when dealing with an open-ended zip.

Advantages: a zip is an easy, smooth fastening, which will not gape, and which goes the length of the opening.
An open-ended zip allows a garment to be opened flat.

Disadvantages: a zip can catch on flesh or clothing underneath, so that a firm fabric backing is advisable.
Where there is strain at the top of zip, e.g. on a waistband, a further fastening may be required.
Back zips are difficult for those with short arms or painful shoulders—a zipaid can be used (see p. 52).
Zips are not suitable for people with jerky, unco-ordinated movements.
When sitting down in a zipped jacket which extends below the waist, the zip tends to bulge or the jacket end to curl up. A two-way zip can help.

If the tag is too small for those with a poor grip it can be enlarged by adding a ring or leather or fabric tag, which makes the tag easier to hold.

Zips can replace laces on shoes; a dressing stick (see p. 46) can pull up the tag.

g *Press studs*

Large and poppa studs should be fixed only to strong firmly woven fabric, or be well backed.

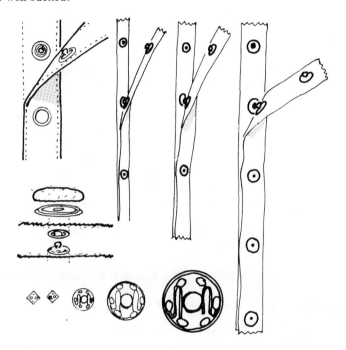

Abilities required for use: pressure is required to put the two parts together. They can be closed one-handed, as long as there is a firm base, such as a bony prominence, or where it is possible to put thumb or forefinger underneath. The greatest power is normally found between the tips of the thumb and finger, but any part of the finger can be used. They can be pulled apart, the smaller size more easily than the larger.

Advantages: they make a neat, flat, invisible fastening.
A button sewn over the top makes a press stud easier to fasten where there is poor grasp or co-ordination.

Disadvantages: they are not suitable where the fastening may be strained.

Large press studs become easier to unfasten once they have been well used.

h *Buckles*

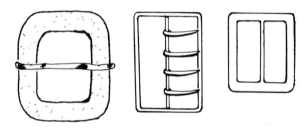

Abilities required for use: the buckle needs to be held still; grasp is required to hold the end of the strap and thread it through the buckle. If the buckle is fixed, for example on a shoe, it can be done up single-handed. A pulling back action is required for unfastening.

Advantages: it is a firm fastening and can be decorative.
Buckles are difficult to undo accidentally.
The buckle without a prong is useful for one-handed people if the free end of the strap is long enough to leave in the buckle while putting the garment on; it can then be pulled to tighten. The end is tucked in.

Disadvantages: small buckles are difficult to manage with poor grasp, co-ordination or sensation.

A buckle with several prongs used with webbing is useful for those with poor co-ordination as there is no need to match up the prong with a hole, but the prongs must lie flat or they will catch on other clothes or on flesh.

The strap should not be pulled too tight.

i *Braces*

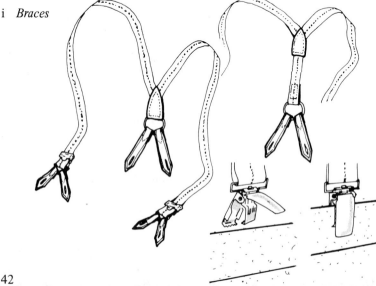

Abilities required for use: braces with loops—finger manipulation to fasten buttons from behind as well as in front.
Braces with clips—enough grip to open clips and release them over the waistband.
It is possible to fasten the braces on to trousers before putting the trousers on, and this can also be done to a skirt.

Advantages: braces may replace a belt.
When held over the arms during toileting, they prevent the trousers from falling down.
They can be used as a dressing aid to pull garments up from the floor.

Disadvantages: clips and buttons can be difficult to do up.

Braces which divide at the shoulder blade level stay on the shoulders better than those dividing at a lower level.
The Turnbull braces may be useful for one-handed people for toileting purposes as there is no need to remove clothes being worn over the top or to undo the braces.

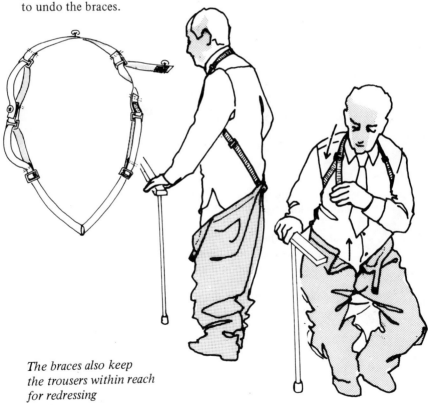

The braces also keep the trousers within reach for redressing

Pants should be attached to the trousers with Velcro so that they can be let down together. To let the trousers down, the Velcro underneath the button is undone (the button prevents the braces from falling); to bring the trousers up, the Velcro is refastened. The unfastened braces should be long enough for the trousers to hang at the base of the buttocks so that the disabled person can easily pull the trousers downwards and to the side when he wishes to sit down. A pattern for the braces is available from the DLF.

j *Suspenders*

Normally used for keeping up stockings or more rarely, for socks.

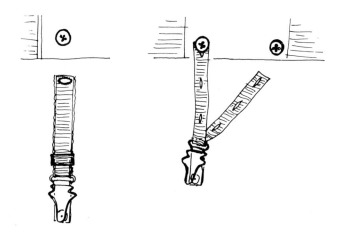

Abilities required for use: the bobble needs to be kept in place underneath the stocking welt while the loop is placed over it and pulled tight.

Advantages: they keep a corset pulled down and stockings up. There are other ways of keeping stockings on and these should be used if doing up suspenders is the only thing preventing complete dressing independence.

Disadvantages: the back suspender can cause pressure when sat upon and should be moved to the side if the disabled person is seated all day. It should be removed altogether if she lacks sensation. Suspenders are difficult to fasten with poor grip, co-ordination or sensation.

44

They can be more easily managed if the suspender can be separated from the garment, attached to the stocking and then re-fastened, for example sew a loop to the suspender and a button on to the garment or use a D-ring or Kempner fastener, sew both suspenders together so that only one loop or hook needs to be done up for front and side suspenders only. Alternatives to suspenders include tights, grip top stockings, socks or pop-socks under trousers, no stockings.

Adaptations of openings and fastenings

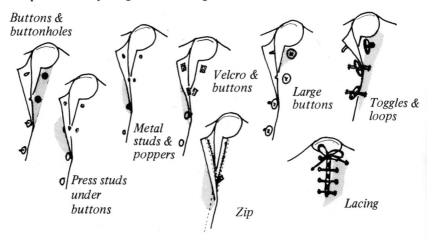

Buttons & buttonholes

Press studs under buttons

Metal studs & poppers

Velcro & buttons

Large buttons

Toggles & loops

Zip

Lacing

Opening seams or changing fastenings can be very helpful for independence and/or dressing more easily: for instance the extension of a trouser fly enables a urinal to be used with improved efficiency when seated.

Dressing Aids

Dressing aids are used to simplify dressing. An aid may be bought or made at home and it can be used in two ways (a) where it is the only solution to a problem for long term use or (b) as a help towards independence, after which it should be discarded where possible. An occupational therapist should be consulted before a dressing aid is provided.

Nurses should be instructed in the use of dressing aids and the circumstances in which they should or should not be used, and should be practised in their use. An understanding of the personality and likely degree of dependence of the disabled person is helpful.

a *Dressing stick*

A hand grip increases the diameter of the stick and may be helpful to those with poor grasp.

The stick should be made to suit the needs of the person using it.

Uses: pick clothes up;
      bring garments round the
       shoulders;
      pull zips up (including shoes);
      tighten or loosen laces;
      push clothes down — pants,
       stockings;
      put stockings/socks over the
       feet and pull them up.

Abilities required: grasp of the hand; some shoulder movement.

Alternatives: the door knob, wall hook, projection of furniture, or corner of a table may help in certain circumstances.

b *Reaching or pick-up aids*

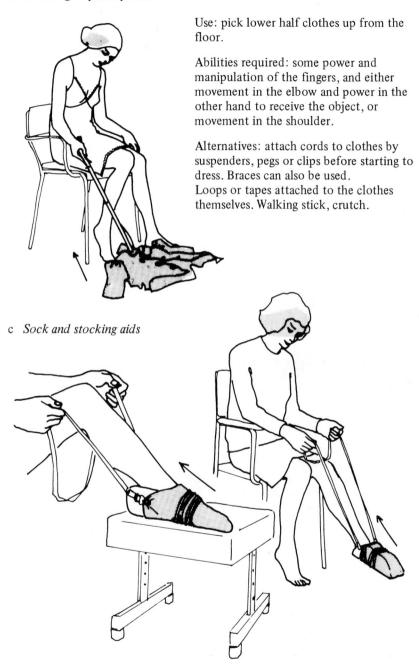

Use: pick lower half clothes up from the floor.

Abilities required: some power and manipulation of the fingers, and either movement in the elbow and power in the other hand to receive the object, or movement in the shoulder.

Alternatives: attach cords to clothes by suspenders, pegs or clips before starting to dress. Braces can also be used.
Loops or tapes attached to the clothes themselves. Walking stick, crutch.

c *Sock and stocking aids*

Abilities required: normally two hands are needed, mobility of spine to lean forward, hands, arms and shoulders to move the aid. Persistence in learning to use it.

Alternatives: some people manage very well with a walking stick.

It is very difficult to advise about putting on elastic stockings, especially by those with weak hands. No aid so far commercially available is suitable as both grip and strength are required to pull the stocking on to the aid.

d *Mirror*

A mirror can remind the dresser of his balance, the look of the garment, the position of fastening and how far on he is with dressing. It also helps to retain a link with reality, reminding him of his own body image.

Dressing is normally taught by the teacher standing in front of the learner so that putting on clothes is learnt via a mirror image (left and right reversed). A mirror enables the teacher to stand behind the learner so that the learner can see the activity for himself and reproduce it more easily. For those with poor sensation, a mirror indicates the position of fastenings, seams, sock heels, etc.

If a mirror increases confusion it should not be used.

Abilities required: sight.

e *Marking clothes*

Use: for those who find it difficult to distinguish concepts such as right and left, inside and outside, and for the blind and partially sighted.

Conceptual difficulties: clothes can be marked with different colours e.g. a right sleeve can be marked with a red dot at the armhole, or a right shoe with a red dot. The left side can be left blank or marked with another colour. Most clothes have a manufacturer's tab at the back and this can be used to teach the concepts of back and front, inside and outside.

Blind people usually develop a compensatory increase in their ability to feel, so that they can be taught to understand the difference between fabrics, shapes and designs; the position of seams; the presence of a manufacturer's tab to denote the back of a garment; identification of matching garments, accessories and colours. The RNIB (Royal National Institute for the Blind) has many useful hints on this.

Disabled people with tetraplegia who cross their feet to put their trousers on may find that they mix up the legs of their trousers, thus putting the garment on back to front. Marking the legs for right and left may therefore be helpful.

The ability to identify colour correctly needs to be tested before colour is used as a marking aid — alternatively a symbol, such as a cross, can be embroidered on the garment.

Dressing can be used as a teaching aid for the right/left concept especially with shoes and gloves.

f *Button hook*

This is a useful aid for those who cannot manage the small movements required to do up buttons, and do not want to alter the fastening.

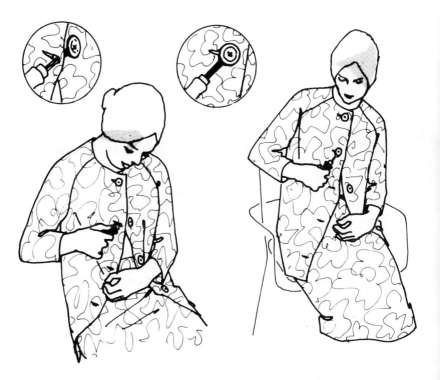

Use: doing up and unfastening buttons.

Abilities required: grip for handle (which can be enlarged), wrist and elbow movement, some eye/hand co-ordination.

g *Loops*

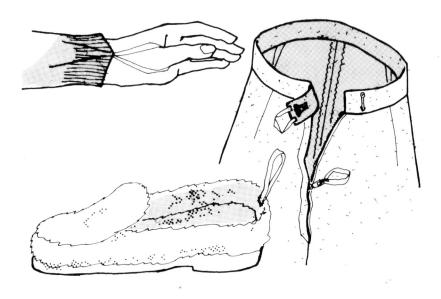

Use: to bring garments nearer to the body or make it easier to do up a fastening.

Abilities required: slip thumb or fingers into the loop or to place the loop over the thumb or finger of the other hand.

h *Elastic laces*

Use: elastic laces enable a disabled person to put on his shoes without bending down. They probably do not give enough support to caliper wearers.

Ability required: must be able to use a shoe horn.

Alternatives: elastic side pieces in the shoes.

i *Shoe horn*

Use: the long handled one
provides an extended length
to those who cannot bend.
They are necessary for
elastic laced or sided shoes.

(Shoe horns should be used
by everyone to prevent the
backs of shoes being
walked down.)

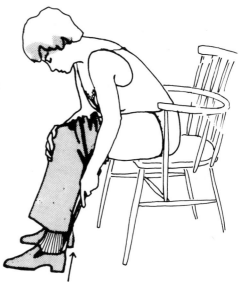

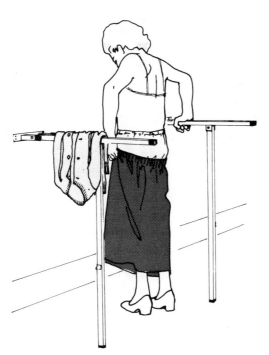

j *Dressing rails*

Use: they give confidence
when standing up to dress.

They can be used as a
clothes valet, but there
must be a clear space for
the hands.

k *Boot remover*

Use: to provide a firm base against which the shoe or boot can be removed.

Alternative: some people manage satisfactorily with the other foot.

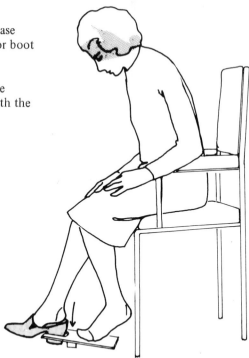

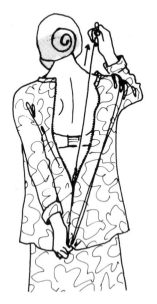

l *Zipaid*

Use: to open and close a zip unaided. To close the zip, the hook of the aid should be inserted into the zip tag before putting on the garment.

Abilities required: some grip to hold the cord; an upward movement of the arm to close the zip; the ability to reach the zip tag at the back of the neck to open it; some method of holding the base of the zip firm.

CHAPTER 6

THE ACTIVITIES OF UNDRESSING AND DRESSING

This chapter has been divided into two sections which look at the activities of undressing and dressing in detail; section 1 undressing and dressing oneself; section 2 being undressed and dressed by a helper. Undressing has been put first as it is usually easier and so should be taught first.

The working illustrations have been divided up according to the type of garment. The same order is used throughout.

Upper half garments: over the head short garments
                                  front opening short garments
                                  back opening short garments

Lower half garments: over the feet
                                  wrap around
                                  hosiery
                                  footwear

Long garments (where not included elsewhere)

Miscellaneous garments

Alterations

Over-the-head short garments

Open-front short garments

Open-back short garments

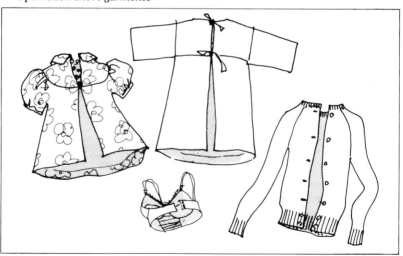

Step-in garments

Open-flat garments

Hosiery

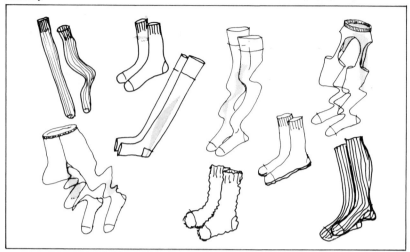

Shoes

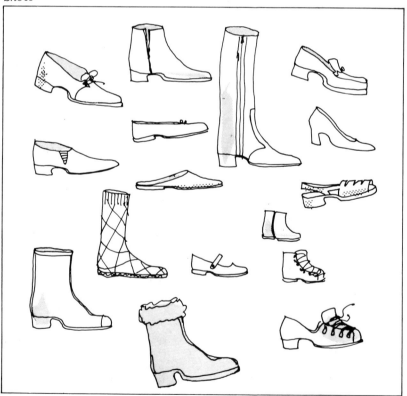

Open front   Open back   Over-the-head

Miscellaneous garments

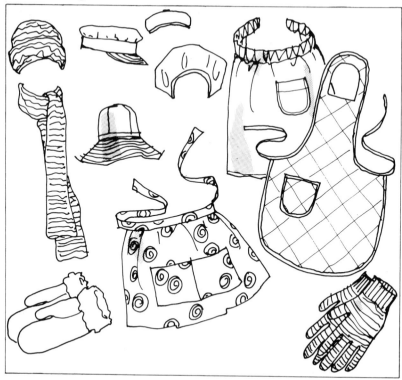

Short garments

Some alterations

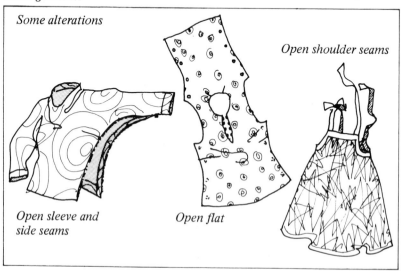

Open sleeve and
side seams

Open flat

Open shoulder seams

Long garments

Some alterations

Bib front

Open side seam

*Open shoulder
and side seams*

Some alterations

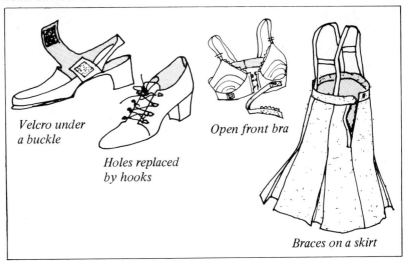

*Velcro under
a buckle*

*Holes replaced
by hooks*

Open front bra

Braces on a skirt

The activity of removing or replacing a garment is made up of many movements but it is usually only possible to show one, or at the most two or three, of these. It is hoped, however, that the illustration used shows a distinctive part. It is not possible to include every variation as each person develops his own way of doing things.

The text of each page is divided up as follows:

Type of garment and method

Position/s in which the activity can be carried out, aids and description of garments as relevant:

a   Positioning of garment etc. prior to activity

b   Description of the activity

c   Any other garments for which the method can be used; variations of method; modifications of garments

d   Contra-indications

Symbols have been used in order to simplify the text and prevent undue repetition.

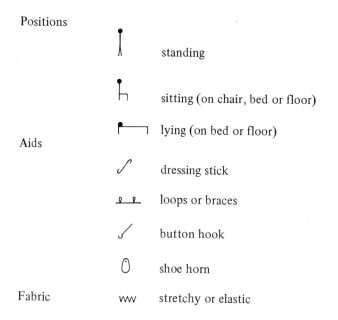

Positions

    standing

    sitting (on chair, bed or floor)

    lying (on bed or floor)

Aids

    dressing stick

    loops or braces

    button hook

    shoe horn

Fabric   stretchy or elastic

A great variety of methods has been included, some more active than others, and it is hoped that this will encourage experimentation. One-handed and tetraplegic methods are included where applicable.

Some general principles

1   Each person should find out the easiest or least painful way by trial and error of putting on and taking off each type of garment (with and without a helper).

2   Support should always be within reach if there is any possibility of falling.

3   With the help of therapists, assessment should be made of the amount of movement a disabled person has, and how pain during dressing can be limited or eliminated.

4   Choice of garment and experimentation with different colours, styles, fabrics, etc should be encouraged.

5   The smallest amount of movement, such as allowing the weight of an arm to pull it down a sleeve, leaning forward in a chair, or bringing the edges of a garment together, should be encouraged.

6   A disabled person can dress or be dressed seated on a flat surface or supported with pillows, or lying on a flat surface (a changing mat on a plinth or the floor for a child, a bed or couch for an adult). Both positions may be used, seated for top and outerwear, lying for underwear.

7   The appropriate part of the body should be supported.

8   The most disabled limb should be dressed first and undressed last.

9   Body supports should be put on before sitting or standing to dress.

10   Calipers should be put on before standing during dressing.

11   An amputee wearing a pylon should first dress the pylon with sock/ stocking, pants and trousers (if worn). After putting the pylon on, the other leg can be dressed followed by the remaining clothes. When undressing the procedure should be reversed.

12   Keep the hair out of the way, if necessary, with a hair net, scarf, headband or shower cap.

13   The correct placing of seams as a garment is put on prevents pulling about afterwards, which may give pain or discomfort and take extra time.

Part 1 — Undressing and dressing oneself

In order to be able to dress oneself completely unaided, the fingers and thumb of one hand should be able to grasp and to reach the feet. A variety of conditions may inhibit this, such as stiffness of the lumbar spine and hips, and/or a thick waistline, which prevent flexion of the trunk and hips; stiffness of the knees, which makes flexion difficult; stiffness of the shoulders, and/or flexed elbows, which prevent the hands reaching the feet; loss of power in hands and arms, including general debility; loss of brain/hand co-ordination; mental handicap; and loss of balance.

Some problems can be overcome or ameliorated by the use of aids, adaptations to clothing, different garments or alternative methods of dressing, or where applicable, such techniques as behaviour modification (see p. 17).

UNDRESSING — UNAIDED

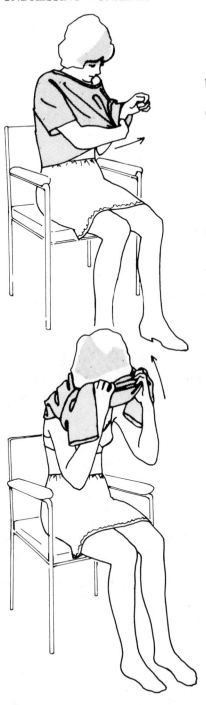

Upper half garments

Over the head — arms first

ⱳⱳ   or good neck opening.

a Sleeves are taken off singly, from the armhole.

b Body of garment is gathered in hands and lifted quickly over head (towards back) from inside.

  Chair arms may support elbows.

c Loose or ample neck opening helpful.

d Contra-indicated for those who lose their balance if the head is covered.

Second Method — crossing arms, bringing garment up over the head.

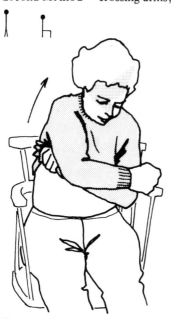

a Cross arms, take hem of garment in each hand.

b Bring up garment over head and shoulders, keeping hands crossed till garment is clear of head.
Let go of garment and strip off sleeves.
Straighten garment.

c Take off stronger arm first, supporting weak arm on table or chair arm.

d Contra-indicated for minimal shoulder movement or short arms with a broad body.

Third Method — garment over back of head first, then arms.

 or slippery garment easiest.

a Grasp sides of neck of garment in each hand.

b Lean forward.
Bring body of garment right over head.
Pull off sleeves from cuff.

c If ⊓ put elbows on table or chair arms.
Gather up back of garment before bringing over the head.

d Contra-indicated for those who become disorientated or may overbalance when head covered or bent.

Fourth Method — garment over front of head first, then arms.

a   Grasp hem at front gathering up garment to armholes.

b   Bring over head.
     Once over head, push sleeves off from the armhole.

d   Contra-indicated with painful shoulder.

Fifth Method — one handed

vvv

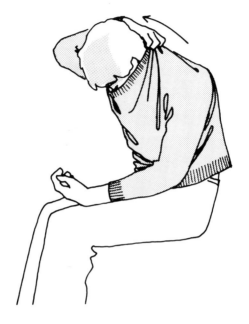

A

a   Hold garment at back of neck, bring collar of garment above nose.

b   Bring garment over back of head and bend neck.
Gather up body of garment at back.
Pull over head, easing sleeve off good arm first by using body.
Remove sleeve from disabled arm.

(For some people it may be easier to remove sleeve from disabled arm first, using teeth at cuff to remove sleeve from good arm.)

c   The disabled arm may be supported on table or chair-arm.

d   Contra-indicated for those with lack of balance.

B

a   Grasp hem on able side with able hand and put elbow into waist of garment.

b   Bring arm up until hand is behind head; bring garment over head and strip sleeve off able arm. Take sleeve off disabled arm.

Front-opening garment

First Method —

A Slip off one shoulder at a time from back.

b With good hand, take opposite sleeve from back.
Pull off, then shake off sleeve from good arm.

d Contra-indicated if backward movement of shoulder is limited.

B Ease sleeves off from armhole.

a Ease sleeve off arm from armhole, starting with whichever arm is easier.

b Pull garment round and remove from other arm.

d Contra-indicated if backward movement at shoulder is limited.

Second Method – Pulling over head.

a Grasp shoulders of garment with
   both hands. For one-handed
   people, grasp back of neck.

b Bend body forward.
   Bring complete garment over
   head.
   When clear of the head, remove
   arms from sleeves.

c Can be used by one-handed
   people.

d Contra-indicated for those with
   limited neck movement.

Third Method –

Use of as aid.

a Undo fastenings, hold lower front
   edges of garment in each hand.

b Lower each shoulder in turn, letting
   sleeve slide down, then pull off by

   cuff, using ⟋ as required.

c Easier with firm or lined garment.
   Front of garment can be reinforced
   by a lining.

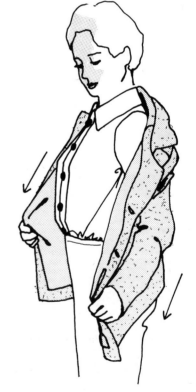

Fourth Method — one handed.

A

a Undo fastenings.

b Bring sleeve of disabled arm well on to shoulder.

c Pull sleeve of good arm off shoulder and arm. Remove sleeve from disabled arm.

B

a Undo fastenings.

b Push shoulders of garment off shoulders.
Grasp centre of front band with good hand, pull back and downwards, ease sleeve off.
Pull sleeve off disabled arm.

c Easier with lined garments.

C

See Second Method p. 68.

Back-fastening garment — slipping sleeves off.

Use of ⟋ as aid.

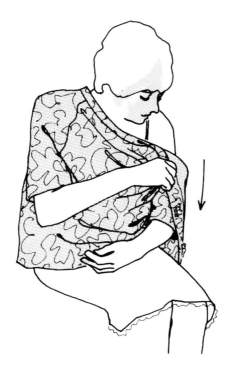

A

a Unfasten.

b Grasp shoulder seam on weaker arm and pull off.
Allow second sleeve to fall off.

B

a For bras.

b Slip straps off shoulders, using ⟋ if required.
Twist garment round, undo fastenings.

Lower half garments

First Method — Trousers, pants, long skirt.

Using 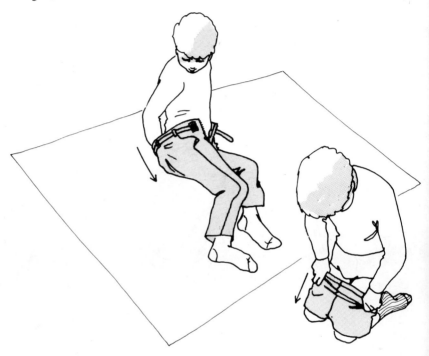 as aid.

a Undo waistband fastening.

b Raise body on one elbow, using arm of chair if

Push down to thigh level, using

Roll on to other side and repeat.

If , sit up to push garment off feet.

If , let it drop off when transferring to bed.

Second Method — Skirt or trousers

Using ₰ ₰ as aid.

a Undo waistband fastening.

b Bring garment down over hips, using ₰ ₰ to hold waistband, and drop.

Bring garment over the hips by rolling.
Bring up one knee, or cross it over other.
Withdraw legs from garment, pushing it off at the same time.

c Holding on to the waistband eliminates bending to pick up the garment later.

Third Method — One handed

Pants, trousers, long skirt

| With or without support

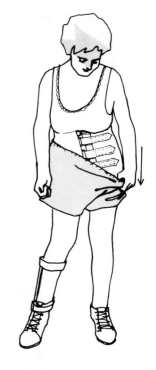

a   Undo fastenings, grasp
     garment with good hand.

b   Push garment down over
     hips.
     Allow to drop off.

c   When taking off trousers,
     remove shoes first.

d   Contra-indicated with
     balancing difficulties.

Fourth Method — Tetraplegic

Trousers, long skirt

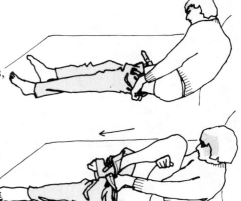

a   Undo waistband.

b   Push garment down over hips,
     rolling from one side to the
     other.
     Raise one knee with hand,
     push down garment.
     Repeat for other leg.

c   When taking off trousers,
     remove shoes first.

     Those with inflexible knees
     may prefer   and push
     garment down to hips, letting
     it fall off when transferring
     to bed.

Hosiery, Socks

First Method —
Pulling on toe of sock.

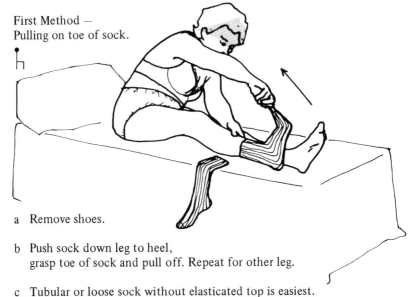

a   Remove shoes.

b   Push sock down leg to heel,
     grasp toe of sock and pull off. Repeat for other leg.

c   Tubular or loose sock without elasticated top is easiest.

Second Method — Socks, stockings or tights
One foot on other knee

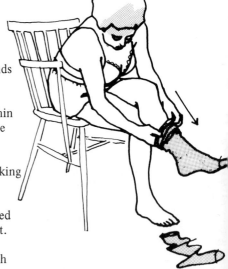

Use walking stick as aid.

a   Remove shoes.
     Cross one leg over other (using hands
     to lift).

b   Put hands on either side of leg within
     the welt of sock/stocking. Continue
     to push until it is removed, with
     walking stick as aid.
     Once it comes over heel, sock/stocking
     can be pulled off by toe.
     Repeat.
     Stockings and tights should be rolled
     down to mid-calf, the good leg first.

c   This process can be carried out with
     one hand, using good hand to push
     down back of sock/stocking.

74

Third Method — One-handed

Socks, stockings, tights

Using a stool as aid.

a   Remove shoes. Raise leg
with good hand,

with foot resting on
stool.

b   Push down sock to ankle and
pull off.
Repeat with other foot.

c   Socks without elasticated
tops are easier to remove.
Stockings and tights should
be rolled down to mid-calf
before pushing down rest of
leg.
For tights, the good leg
should be undressed first.
Avoid struggling with the
head bent.

Shoes

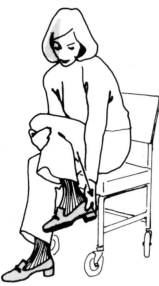

First Method — Raising and supporting knee.

Using stool as aid.

a   Undo fastenings.
    Use stool to bring foot nearer body, or cross knees.

b   Remove shoe or boot with free hand.

c   Boots should be opened well out before removing.

Second Method — Using other foot.

a   Undo laces or fastenings.

b   Put one foot behind the other and push shoe off.

c   A boot remover can also be used (p. 52).

d   Contra-indicated with one disabled foot/leg.

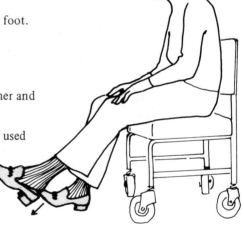

Third Method — Low-cut slip-on shoes or slippers can be taken off by contracting toes and raising heel within the shoe.

To undo fastenings.

Bend knee and put foot on chair, kneel down or bend knee and support it on chair to bring foot near to hip.

Over-the-head garment (long)

Roomy garment with side or back waist opening, petticoat or garment without sleeves.

ᴡᴡ

a Unfasten.
Cross arms and grip garment at hips.

b Pull garment upwards and over head, uncrossing the arms.
Strip off sleeves.

c Contra-indicated for those with limited or painful shoulder movement, lack of grip, balance or stiff neck.

Letting garment drop to feet

Using ⌒ or Zipaid if required.

For petticoat, back or front half-open garments.

a Undo fastenings, if any, using Zipaid if required.

b Pull sleeves or straps down

arms using ⌒

⌐ Let slip off. Step out.

⊓ Leave garment at hip level until moving from chair to bed, or roll from side to side to push it off.

Wrap-around garments

Removing a corset/corselette

a Unfasten starting from bottom, one
hand holding side steady.

b Complete unfastening and remove.

Leave garment on chair when
transferring to bed.

Roll off garment.

For corselette, one bra strap must be undone or
taken over the head to complete undressing.

c Hooks and eyes may be replaced by D-ring
or Kempner fastener.

Dressing or Undressing

Getting a garment over hips by rolling.

Suitable for dress, skirt, trousers, pants.

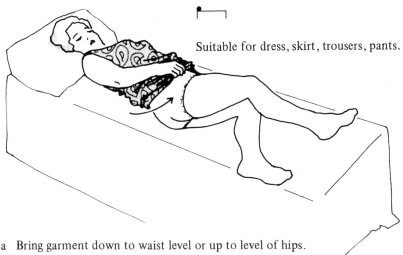

a Bring garment down to waist level or up to level of hips.

b Roll on one side and bring garment down/up (see p. 101).
Repeat for other side.

d Contra-indicated where the patient is unable to twist the body at waist.

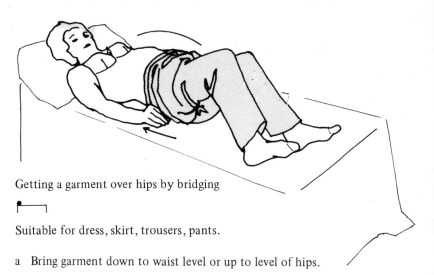

Getting a garment over hips by bridging

Suitable for dress, skirt, trousers, pants.

a   Bring garment down to waist level or up to level of hips.

b   Bend knees, dig feet into surface, raise hips. Bring garment down/up.

d   Contra-indicated with inability to raise hips from bed, or general weakness.

Getting garment over hips by shifting in chair.

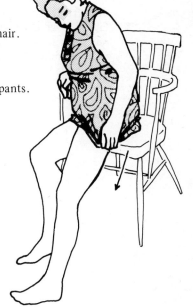

Suitable for dresses, long skirts, trousers, pants.

a   Put garment on over head or over legs, or bring up to thighs.

b   Turn from side to side using arms of chair as support, bracing foot on opposite side on floor exposing the hips.

Pull garment up or down, as appropriate.

DRESSING — UNAIDED

Over-the-head garments

First Method — Head first, followed by arms.

a Place garment front downwards, neck opening furthest away.

b Pull garment over head. First arm in (weaker arm first).
Arrange shoulder and sleeve seams so these are correctly placed once garment is on.
Repeat for second arm. Pull down back of garment.

c To reduce need for shoulder activity place elbows on chair arms or table.

If ⌐—⌐ roll from side to side or sit up to pull down back of garment.
Large neck openings are useful with disorientation, overbalancing and large heads.

d Contra-indicated for those with disorientation or overbalancing when face is covered; those with one weak arm, limited shoulder movements, or one handed.

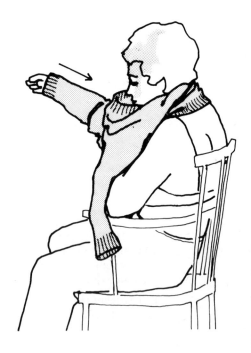

Second Method – Arms before head

ww   Front opening garment, or no fastening bra.

a   Place garment front downwards, neck opening furthest away.

b   Thread first arm into sleeve (weaker arm first) as far as possible, resting on table or chair arm. Gather back of garment in hands, raise the arms, bring garment over head, straighten neck, bring elbows back to pull garment down.

c   If [symbol] roll from side to side or sit up to pull down back of garment.

d   Contra-indicated for those with stiff neck.

Third Method – Weaker arm first, followed by head and second arm.

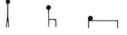

ww   or no-fastening bra.

a   Head bent or straight. Place garment downwards, neck opening furthest away.

b   Thread weaker arm into sleeve. Straighten sleeve and shoulder seams.
    Bring garment over head. Put second arm in. Straighten seams.

c   If [symbol] roll from side to side or sit up to pull down back of garment.

Fourth Method — One-handed (Third Method also possibly suitable)

⌐

ww   or one size too large

a Place garment downwards, neck
   opening away from body.

b Pick up garment at hem,
   supporting disabled arm on
   table or chair arm. Pull garment
   over head. (The body of the
   garment can be gathered as far
   as neck.)
   Place disabled arm in sleeve,
   pull on and adjust.
   Repeat for second arm,
   adjusting by pushing sleeve
   downwards against body.

c Long sleeves on able arm should have no-fastening cuffs — eg - elasticated
   or stretchy material used instead.

Fifth Method — Over head for no-fastening or fastened bra.

This method requires a well-elasticated and short-length bra. Fourth Method may be easier.

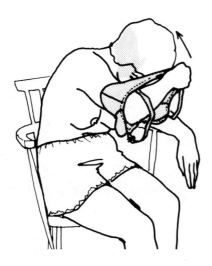 as aid.

a   Check bra is right-side out, with cups facing forward.

b   Put arms into bra to above elbows. Lift back of bra over the head, resting elbows on table or chair arms. Pull down and settle, using

c   Adjustable straps can be loosened before dressing and tightened afterwards.

d   Contra-indicated for those with limited shoulder movement, weak hands or stiff cervical or thoracic spine.

Short front-opening garments

First Method — Weaker arm in, garment brought round back, second arm in.

or walking stick as aids

a Hold garment by shoulder above
   sleeve to be put on first.

b Thread first (weaker) arm on as
   far as shoulder. Straighten seams.

   or walking stick can bring
   rest of garment round the back.
   Bringing the first sleeve well up
   on to shoulder prevents it falling
   back when putting in second arm.
   Put arm into second armhole.
   settle sleeves. Fasten.

c A garment with fullness at back makes pulling on second sleeve easier.
   A slippery lining on an outer garment is easier to put on.
   To fasten, if co-ordination is limited, use a mirror to start the fastening
   process at the bottom and work up.
   Make into an over-the-head garment by fastening it at the bottom.

   The second arm can be put into the sleeve at waist level.

d Contra-indicated for those with limited movement in both shoulders.

Second Method — Putting both sleeves on, raising arms to bring garment over the head. This avoids crossing arms or putting one behind the back.

ww   Easiest with lined or larger size garment.

a   Garment placed inside outwards, collar nearest body.

On lap if ⌐ , on table or

chair if |

b   Put arms into sleeves above elbows. Bend head, raise arms and bring garment over head. Allow sleeves to slip down the arms.

c   If shoulder movements are limited, ensure sleeves seams are straight and that sleeves reach shoulders before raising arms. Bend elbows when bringing garment over head.

A split garment or with fullness at back makes dressing easier.

d   Contra-indicated for stiff painful shoulders, and for heavy garments.

Third Method — Garment, inside outwards, supported on *high-backed* chair, allowing both arms to be placed in sleeves. Small shoulder movements only required.

Use

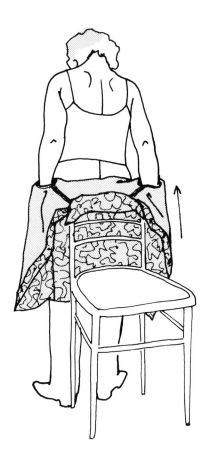

a   Place garment inside outwards over back of chair, shoulders at top, lean forward.

If   then garment is similarly placed over *front* of chair-back, pushing any free fabric to back of chair seat.

b   Bend knees slightly to enable arms to slip into sleeves.

   Put arms into sleeves.

Bring up on to shoulders with opposite hands.

Settle sleeves on shoulders using   to help bring garment up.

c   This method can be used with one hand.

Fourth Method — Garment swung round shoulders as normally used for cape, but can be used, even with one weak arm, for front-opening garments with sleeves.

a Hold garments by fronts of collar or neckband.

b Swing round, settle on shoulders and hold end of collar/neckband with stronger hand. Put arm into sleeve. Put second hand in other sleeve. Complete dressing.

c Lean forward to let the back of garment drop down to complete dressing.
With one weak arm see p. 107.

d Contra-indicated if both shoulders are weak.

Fifth Method — One-handed

 or larger size.

a Put sleeve on to disabled arm.

b Pull up on shoulder to neck. Straighten seams. Rest of garment should hang down centre back. Bring second sleeve to able side by bringing collar round back of neck and placing garment on to shoulder. Put in arm, adjust and fasten.

c Difficult if neck is low cut.

Back-fastening garments

First Method — Drawing sleeves on

Garments should be loose-fitting. Also for full-length open-back garment.

a Grasp garment at shoulder
of weaker arm of sleeve to be
put on first.

b Pull up, straighten shoulder
seam. Put on second sleeve,
repeat. Fasten.

c   Weaker arm can be supported on chair arm. Some disabled people
may require help with fastenings.

d Contra-indicated with regard to fastening if shoulder movement is limited,
hands and/or fingers weak or unco-ordinated, arms are short.

88

Second Method

A Putting on a back fastening bra, fastening it at front and swinging it round to back.

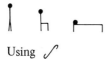

Using ⟋

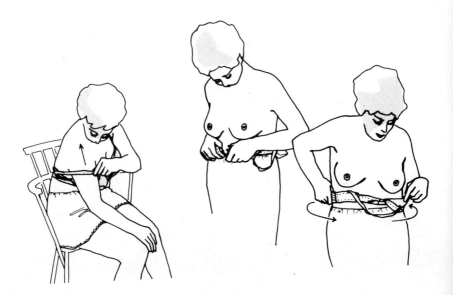

a Bring bra round body at waist level.

   If ⌐ use ⟋ to push garment under body.

b Fasten, and swing round to back. Put arms into straps. Pull up straps,

   using ⟋ if required.

c ⌐   There is a natural hollow at waist-level which makes pushing
   bra round easier. Broad straps stay more easily on shoulders. Elastic straps
   can be used to anchor other straps by tucking them underneath.

d Contra-indicated unless elastic straps, or adjustable straps of sufficient
   length, are used.

B As for **A**, but one-handed.

Using

a Bring bra round body at waist-level, using   , using disabled arm/hand to anchor it.

b Fasten and proceed as in **A**.

c Elastic or part-elastic straps are necessary. Sew back fabric under hooks for easier fastening.

d Contra-indicated if disabled arm/hand cannot be used in any way.

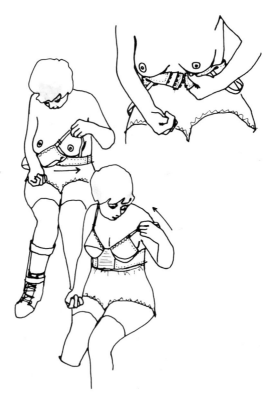

C Where disabled hand cannot be used, wear front-fastening bra with Kempner fastener or Velcro and D-ring at bottom edge of bra which, once fastened, enables hooks or other fastenings to be done up with one hand.

Lower-half garments

First Method — Over the feet.

Use of ♀ ♀ and ∫ as aids.

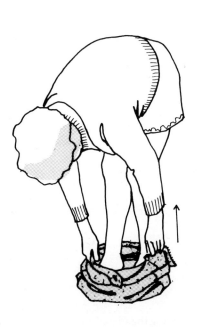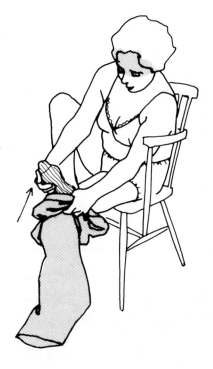

a Hold garment by waistband, making sure it is positioned correctly for wear, and drop garment to floor.

b Bend over and insert feet.

   Bring up to waist, using ∫ for ♀ ♀

   Either stand and pull up garment or turn from side to side. Fasten securely.

c Can be used for trousers, skirt or underclothing.

   If ⊓ , feet may be placed on a stool.

d Contra-indicated for those with stiff hips or short arms with a heavy body.

Second Method — Throwing garment beyond feet where it is supported by bed or floor before dressing normally.

Using rope ladder, ⟋ and ๏ ๏ as aids.

b Sit up and pick-up garment by waistband and flick it forward to be neatly in front.
Draw over feet and bring it up over legs, using ⟋ and ๏ ๏ if required.
Roll from side to side or bridge hips to bring garment up to waist.
Fasten.

c With painful side-hip movement, put a bandage or towel under the leg and use it as a sling to move leg sideways.
This can also be used to lift the leg upwards.
Poor sitting balance may be aided by use of rope ladder or by support given by pillows or back rest.
To reduce the movements required the garment can be left below the hips until transfer to a chair takes place.

An open-flat garment may be easier to roll on to.

d Contra-indicated for those with poor sitting balance.

One-handed method — over-the-feet.

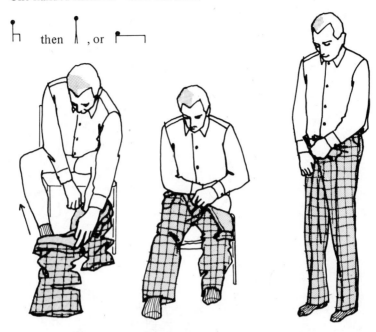

a ⌐∩ Hold garment by waistband, making sure it is positioned correctly for wear, and drop garment to floor. If ⌐—⌐ , sit up.

b Bend over and insert feet.

⌐ and bring up to waist, using disabled hand/arm or braces to keep up waistband during fastening.

If the disabled hand/arm is unable to keep up the waistband, either sit down again after bringing garment over hips, or if ⌐—⌐ roll from side to side to bring garment over hips.

c Poor balance can be helped by leaning against a solid piece of furniture or dressing on a bed.

Braces will keep trousers up while fastening the waistband.

Waistband fastenings should be adapted where necessary with a buckle, Velcro or large hook and bar.

d Contra-indicated for those with poor balance.

Hosiery (socks, stockings, tights)

Use sock or stocking gutter, or stool as aids.

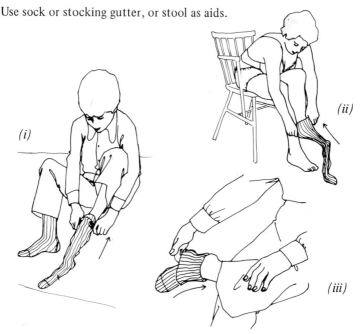

(i)

(ii)

(iii)

a Hold sock open between both thumbs lined up with foot. Heel of sock underneath. (Illustration i)
One knee over the other, sock open between both thumbs (Illustration ii).
Double sock over, place on foot as far as heel (Illustration iii).

b Pull on, and up leg, straightening as required.

c Tights are pulled on, each leg separately, as far as thighs, then pull up to waist or ⌐‾‾⌐ roll from side to side.
For stiff hips bring foot up to the side of the hip.
A heel-less sock/stocking is useful where co-ordination is poor, or in cases of severe mental handicap.
Socks with a separate big toe/toes are available for those who use their feet in lieu of hands.

d Contra-indicated with stiff hips or immobile spine.

For use of gutters, see p. 47.

Second Method — One-handed

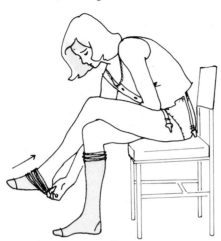

Use ✓ , walking stick or stool as aids.

a Support weak leg on opposite
   knee (and/or stool) and gather up
   sock/stocking as far as foot, with
   thumb inside.

b Place stocking on foot and bring
   it up the leg, pulling on alternate
   sides or at back and smoothing
   with the palm of the hand as well
   as fingers.

   Fasten suspenders.

c ✓ and walking stick can be
   used as aids to drop sock/
   stocking on to foot and bring
   it up the leg.

Knee-high or above knee socks/stockings eliminate need for suspenders.
A stool reduces the amount of bending required.

d Contra-indicated with immobility of spine.

Doing up suspenders — one-handed method

a Put on stockings and suspender belt.
   Choose best position where there is
   minimal strain on the suspender and
   stocking welt.

b Slip button of suspender under
   stocking top and steady it against
   the thigh.
   Use thumb and forefinger to push
   slide over button and pull up.

c Stay-up stockings or tights avoid
   need for suspenders.

d Contra-indicated with poor finger
   movement.

Shoes

First Method — slip-on shoe

Stool or ⵔ may be used as aid.

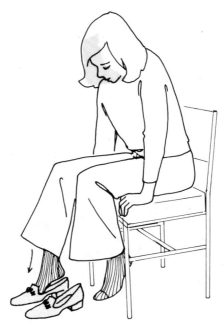

a   Place shoes in front of feet, straps (if any) undone.

b   Ease foot into shoe, using ⵔ

    Put on second shoe.

c   Long-handled ⵔ minimises bending, as does a footstool, which is
    more convenient if the top is angled.

    A slip-on shoe can give good support if there are elasticated panels.

    A strap shoe with buckles may give as much support as laces.

d   Contra-indicated where a supportive shoe is required.

Second Method — Lace-up shoes/boots

Use 𝙾 and ╱ as aids

a For ease of dressing, shoes are normally put on after trousers.
Open out lace-up shoes as far as possible, pull out tongue of shoe.

⊓ Support the leg over opposite knee.

b Ease the shoe over foot, using 𝙾

╎ Bend over, put foot into shoe using longhandled 𝙾
Tie laces.

c Boots should be put on with both hands where possible. A loop at the
back of an ankle boot helps in pulling on.

Laces can be replaced by hooks (as used on climbing or ski-boots) or by a

zip, which can be closed using ╱

Those with poor sensation in feet should have shoes/boots which allow the
position of the toes to be checked.

Third Method — One-handed

Using $\mathring{0}$ and ✓

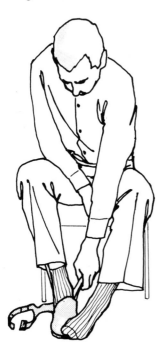

a Place shoes in front of feet. Laced shoes should be undone and well open.

b Place weaker foot in shoe, using able foot to anchor it.

   Use $\mathring{0}$ to ease on.

   Place other foot in second shoe, using $\mathring{0}$.

   Fasten shoes. Buckles can be fastened with one hand while laces require a special technique of lacing (see below).

c Laces can be replaced by Velcro or by hooks (as in climbing or ski-boots).

   If elastic laces are used, the tongue should be stitched to the shoe on one side to prevent "rucking".

One-handed method of lacing and fastening.

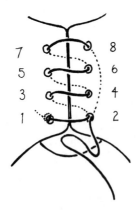

Remove metal tag of lace, make a knot and threat up through 1. Thread down through 2, up through 3 and so on to 8. Thread back from 8 up through 2, leaving a long end. To fasten, tighten the lace from the top towards the toe and then pull at long end. Make a loop, pass it under the top lacing and tighten.

✓   can be used throughout.

Putting on wrap-round garment (skirt, corsets)

First Method — One-handed

a   Use one hand to anchor garment at side.

b   Bring rest of garment round body. Fasten.

Second Method — lying

a   Lay the garment open on bed.

b   Roll on to it. Fasten.

c   Corsets may be put on   or   . Surgical corsets should only be put on lying flat. Kempner fasteners or Velcro with a D-ring are useful for one-handed people.

Third Method

a Place garment loosely in chair, inside uppermost, with sides overlapping arms of chair.

b Sit down, pull around, fasten; adjust garment.

Putting on trousers or long skirt — tetraplegic with flexible knees and hips

Using ⟋ as aid.

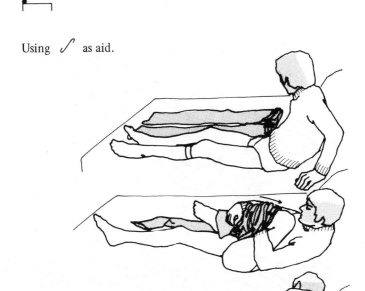

a Put trousers (or skirt) right side up on bed beside lower half of body.

b Lift one leg with hand, ease on leg of trousers with wrist of other arm.
Repeat.
Roll over on side and pull up.
Repeat and fasten (see p. 104) using ⟋

c (Pillows give support behind). A chair with arms beside the bed may
be useful.
A long skirt is very suitable for a woman as it enables her to wear socks
and conceals a urine bag (if used).

A wrap-around skirt can be rolled into.

d Contra-indicated for inflexible knees (see p. 102).

Tetraplegic with inflexible knees — trousers

Using 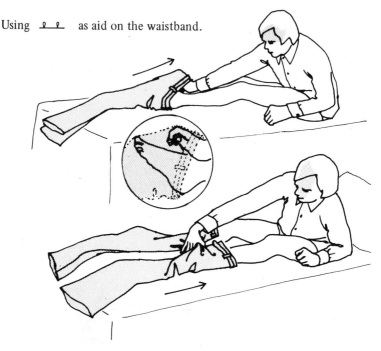 as aid on the waistband.

a Place trousers at end of bed adjacent to stockinged feet.

b Pull opened trousers under heels with whatever grip remains (see inset)

   by raising heels and using ♀ ♀ .
   Ease up the legs by alternatively pushing garment under heels and pushing up the legs.
   Once trousers are at hip level, roll from side to side to bring them up.

   Fasten (p. 104).

c Crossing the feet may help to raise the heels — in this case care must be taken to position trouser legs correctly.

   (Balance may be regained by rope ladder.)

   Zips in the inner seams may make trousers easier to put on as there is less to pull under heels. They should be undone before starting to dress.

Waistband fastenings (trousers, long skirt, corset, trousers)

Using ⟋ , ᴒ ᴒ (with hook and bar) or ⟋

First Method

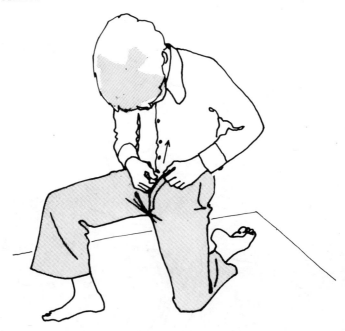

a Bring ends of waistband together.

b Do up fastening. Use ⟋ to pull up zip.

c Buttons may be replaced by Velcro on either side of an extended zip, or by trouser hook and bar.

    Loop on end of waistband (p. 50) can help poor finger movement –

    pull ᴒ ᴒ so the trouser hook is well beyond bar, then allow to slip back.

    Use ⟋ where grip is poor.

d Contra-indicated with poor grip or finger movement.

Second Method — Poor grip or finger movement

Using  , ⌒ ⌒ , ⌐ as aids.

a Bring end of waistband together using fingers as shown.

b Do up zip, using ⌐ . Do up belt, using ⌐ to do up buttons and
⌐ to close zip.

c An enlarged zip pull may be helpful, or replace zip by Velcro.

d Contra-indicated where finger co-ordination is poor.

Over-the-head long garments

Arms first, followed by head.

ww   or with good opening at side, front or back, extending below waist.

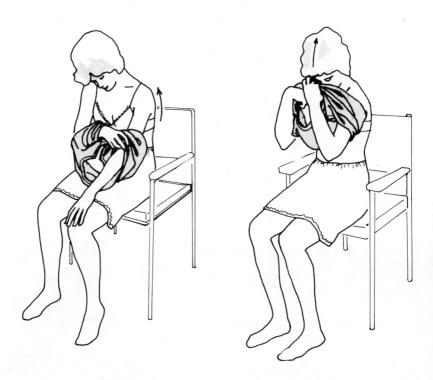

a Gather up skirt with both hands through neck opening.

b Put arms in sleeves, pulling well up on to shoulders. Elbows on table or chair arms reduces need for shoulder activity. Pull over head. Adjust seams.

skirt will drop

roll from side to side to bring skirt down.

c Large neck openings are useful for those with large heads, or where disorientation or overbalancing is a problem.

Stepping into half-open back garment

Using Zipaid

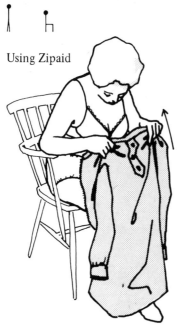

a Make a ring of garment to step into.

b Step into garment. Put feet in to garment and draw it up to knees. Roll to bring over hips.

Pull up to slip over shoulders and arms.

Settle seams. Fasten, using Zipaid for zip.

c Fastening is difficult for those with short arms, poor co-ordination or shoulder movements (below).

Half-open back long garment

Garment should open well below waist.

a Bring whole garment over the head and arms and drop garment to waist.

b Insert arms into armholes, pull up to shoulders. Settle on to shoulders and fasten. Roll from side to side to bring skirt down or stand to allow it to drop.

c Can also be used for half-open front long garment.

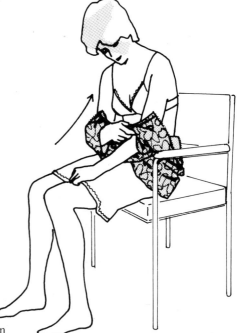

Putting on open-fronted garment

a Put weaker hand in sleeve and bring well up on to shoulder.

b Put other hand on edge of collar.
Swing garment round. Put second hand in sleeve.

Fasten, ⌐ or roll to pull down over hips.

c Open dress or skirt may also be sat in.
Can be done one-handed.

One-handed Method — For garment opening in front below waist.

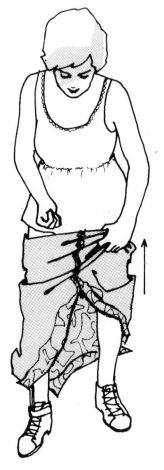

Using pick-up stick as aid.

a   Undo fastenings.

Hold garment so that a clear circle may be seen to step into.

b   Step into circle. Pick garment up, bring to waist and use disabled arm to steady it.

Put feet in circle, bend to pick up garment using pick-up stick and pull

garment to hips.   to pull over hips or roll from side to side.
Draw sleeve on to disabled arm.
Push arm into second sleeve.

c   Doubling the bodice over the skirt may be helpful.
Support where required may be provided either by leaning against wall or by putting on shoes first.
If the opening stops at waist, open the waist seam to the side seam on disabled side, and then for several inches down the side seam, using Velcro as fastening.

Additional Garments

Gloves — one-handed

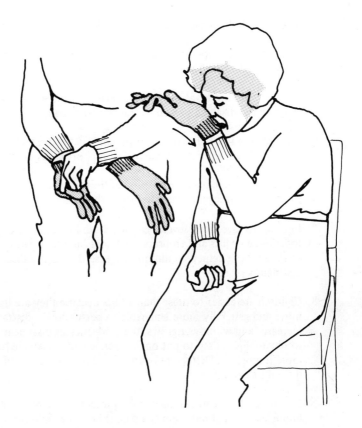

a   Place gloves in position on thighs.

b   Pull glove on to disabled hand with able hand.
    "Crawl" able hand into second glove, pull wrist of glove down with teeth.

c   Gloves must be flexible. Mittens or a muff may be easier.
    Wrist of glove on able hand may require strengthening.

Part 2 — being undressed and dressed by a helper

There are a number of points worth emphasising with regard to helping someone to undress and dress.

1 Use of dressing as passive physiotherapy wherever possible.

2 The helper's movements should be made firmly, smoothly and gently.

3 Discovery of the ways the disabled person likes to be dressed, how his helper has dressed him, the movements likely to induce spasm (see p. 22-23).

4 Furniture should be at the correct height for the helper and be adjustable to allow the disabled person to transfer to a chair.

5 The helper will be able to use both hands if the disabled person is supported, but only one if she has to support limbs or head.

6 The helper should plan the position of the disabled person and the furniture, to give the former the least strain and the minimum of movement.

7 In order to save time, several garments can be put on and then adjusted together, eg pants and trousers, petticoats and long garment, but the saving of time by the helper should not increase the pain or discomfort of the disabled person.

8 Children are easier to dress than adults because they are lighter, easier to move and generally more amenable to persuasion or distraction. As weight increases and willpower grows, these advantages disappear and clothes which are light, easy to put on, attractive and adjustable become even more important. Deliberate resistance to dressing and undressing is difficult to counteract.

N.B. Children with cerebral palsy may present severe problems. It is important to find out from the parent how the child is normally handled, and always to continue with this method. There are four or five methods of therapy, and each of them must be practised continuously if the child is to gain the maximum benefit. Carrying, dressing, seating and placing the child are normally included — all are important, and are no more difficult to use than the usual methods (see Finnie, N. *Handling the young cerebral palsied child at home* and pamphlets issued by the Spastics Society and Friends of the Centre for Spastic Children (App. III).)

UNDRESSING – AIDED

Upper half garments – long or short

First method – sleeves off, then overhead.

ww   or half-open back.

a   Gather up garment to first armhole, stronger arm first. (A long garment should first be brought over hips).

b   Take off sleeve helped by weight of arm.
Repeat for second sleeve.
Gather garment up and take over head.

c   If the person is unable to help himself, pull armhole down as far as elbow and ease arm and hand through.
Grasp garment at hem and pull straight upwards taking sleeves off with the upward movement.

Second method — First arm, head, second arm

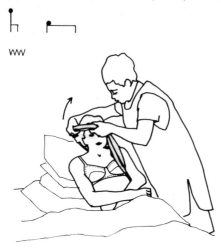

a Bring garment up to armholes.

b Slip off one sleeve.
Gather up garment and bring over head.
Draw off other sleeve.

Front opening garment

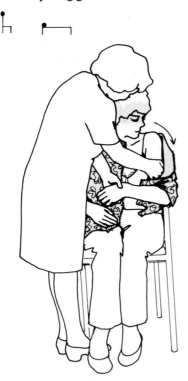

a Unfasten. Bend elbow of one arm, pull fabric down with fingers.

b Ease arm out.
Bring garment round back.
Draw off second sleeve.

⌐ Alternatively, roll on one side, bring one arm back and bring sleeve down on arm. Tuck garment into back and roll on to other side.

⌐ Raise neck of garment and ease out first arm from back.

or Pull neckband of garment towards sleeve to be taken off.

or Pull back of garment away from body, easing sleeve down arm which have been drawn back.

or Bring garment off both shoulders before easing first sleeve off.

c ⌐ is contra-indicated for stiff/painful shoulders.

Open-back garment

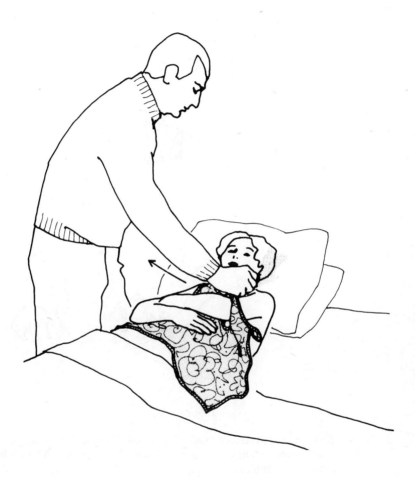

a Roll to one side.

b Unfasten, push edges of garments to sides.
   Roll back.
   Draw off each sleeve in turn.

Lower half garments

First Method − Rolling person by two people.

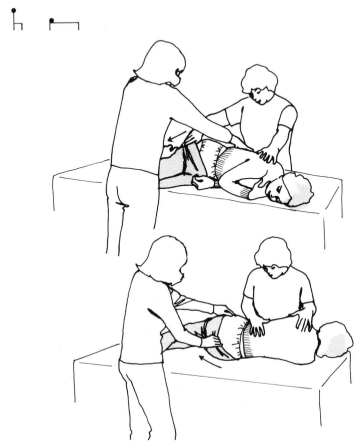

a Head well supported or head lying on side. Garment unfastened.
First person puts hands on buttocks and shoulders, second with hands
on mid-back and lower thigh.

b Roll person over, pulling down garment over hips.
Roll person over to other side, pulling garment down and over feet.

Roll person from side to side or raise from seat of chair to bring
garment off the hips.
Ease rest of garment off.

c A pillow can be placed under head.

114

Second Method — Pushing garment down legs.

(An example of self-help where child must be kept in balance)

⌐‾‾⌐ (on floor)

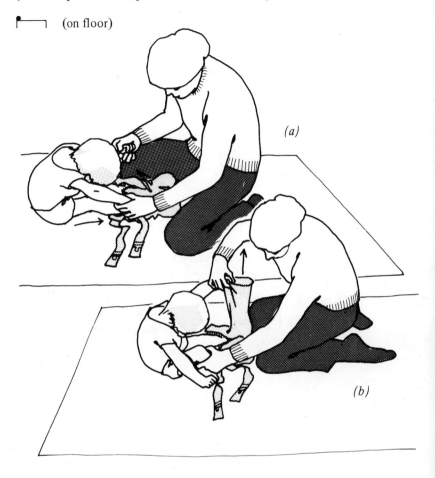

(a)

(b)

a Undo fastenings. Kneel (note position of helper's knees, enclosing the child's feet very firmly — to keep in balance) holding child's hands.

b Pull child up and forward and roll garment off hips.
   Hold on to one hand to keep him forward.
   Encourage child to push trouser legs down (a) and then to pull off (b), keeping child forward.

Shoes

Removing shoes/slippers/boots

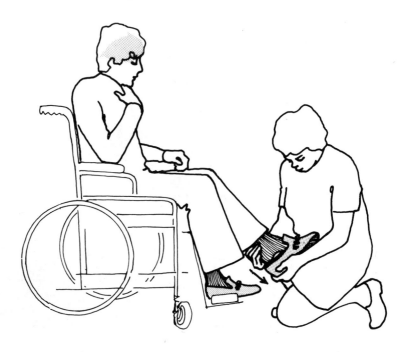

a Completely open out fastenings with foot at rest.

b Support ankle with one hand, pull down shoe by heel with the other.

c Note any areas of inflammation on foot or holes in hosiery where shoe may be rubbing.

Corsets

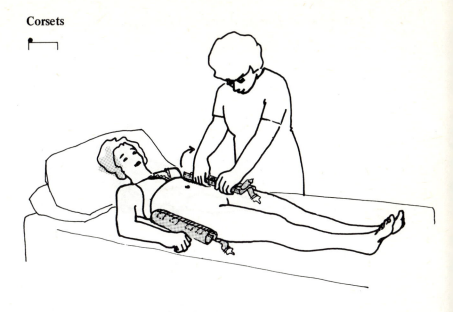

a Unfasten completely — person lies on flat surface.

b Take edges of corset to sides and tuck in one edge, right to person's side. Roll person to that side and remove garment.

c Roll-on corsets can be taken off only if the person can stand or be rolled easily from side to side.
Step-in corsets should be unfastened and brought down over legs.

Half-open back garment — take off to the hips downwards.

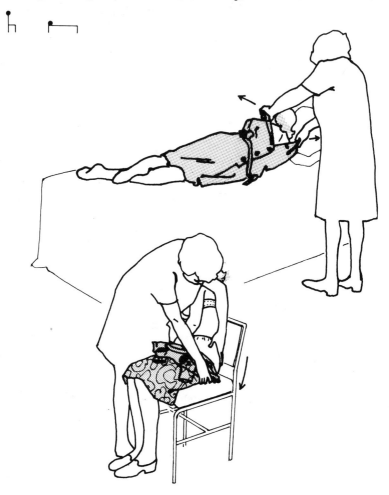

a Roll person to one side. Unfasten garment.

b Push edges of garment to appropriate sides.
    Ease off top sleeve.
    Roll over.
    Ease off other sleeve.
    Pull garment over hips and legs.

c The garment can also be removed by bringing it up over the hips, sitting
    person up and taking it off over the head.

118

Open-front garment

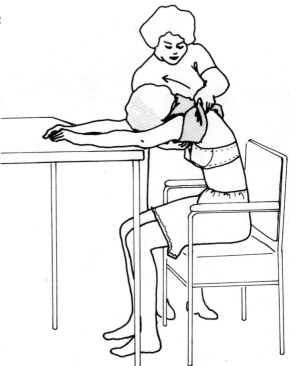

a   Undo fastenings.

b   Push garment off
    shoulders.
    Hold first arm and
    ease out of sleeve.
    Repeat with second
    arm.

    leave on chair or

    roll over to
    remove skirt.

Over-the-head garment

ᴡᴡ   or sleeveless
garment

a   Free the skirt of
    the garment and
    bring over hips.

b   Rest arms on
    support.

    Bring garment up
    to armholes, ease
    arms out and lift
    garment over head
    from back.

c   Garment must
    be ᴡᴡ , loose
    fitting or sleeve-
    less with good
    neck opening.

DRESSING – AIDED

First Method – head first then arms.

Suitable for long or short garments.

ww   or half open front – or back-fastened garment.

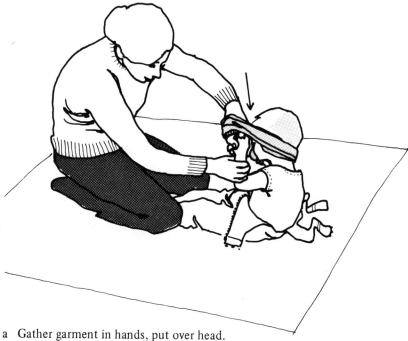

a   Gather garment in hands, put over head.

b   Place shoulder seams correctly.
Blend the arm at elbow and either put hand into armhole or thread own hand through sleeve, grasp person's hand and bring down sleeve.
Pull sleeve up and adjust.
Repeat with second arm.

⌐¬ Sit up or roll to pull garment down body and smooth out creases.

c   A fixed elbow is easier to dress by Second or Third Methods.
Long garment is most easily put on sitting up.
Good neck openings help in getting garment over head.

Second Method — arms first then head.

ww   or sleeveless

Short or long garments

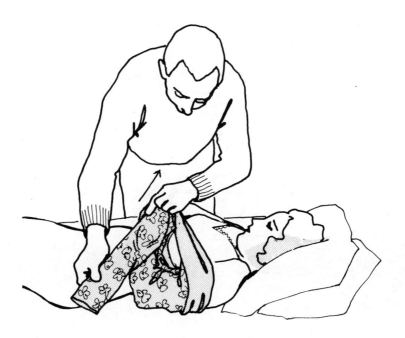

a Put in arms by chosen method, bring up to armholes.

b Gather back of garment in hands, lift and bring over head, supporting it until garment is round neck.

⌐┐ Sit up or roll person to bring garment down.

c A fixed elbow may be more easily coped with if the sleeve seam is opened.

Third Method — one arm in, then head, then second arm

ww   or good neck opening.

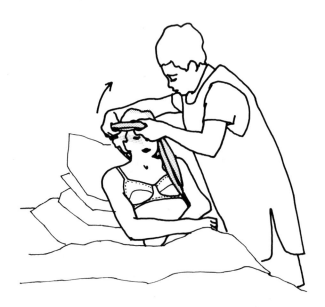

a   Thread first arm on by chosen method.

b   Gather garment up at neck and place over head.
    Put in second arm.
    Adjust seams.

    Sit up or roll to pull garment down.

Fourth Method — Front Opening Garment — one sleeve on, with garment brought round the back (long or short).

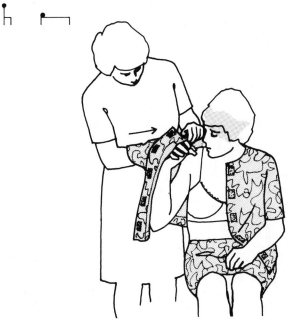

a First sleeve in.

b Bring garment high up on the shoulder.
  Adjust seams.
  Bring round the back, raise armhole to above shoulder level.
  Bend elbow of second arm, thread into sleeve.
  Pull up.

  If ⌐¬ roll over or sit up.

  Do up fastenings.

  Alternatively,
  Garment is brought round back.
  Second armhole brought as low as possible, second sleeve put on with arm pointing downwards.

c A firm garment such as sports or suit jacket can be split up back seam (fastened with Velcro or zip) to help in bringing it round the back, for shoulders too stiff or painful for above method.
  Additional fullness in back gives extra aid.

123

Fifth Method — Both sleeves, then over head, backwards.

ʰ ⌐

ᴡᴡ roomy or sleeveless garment.

a Garment placed downwards, hem to body.

b Thread on sleeves.
Support the arms.
Gather garment and lift over head.
Bring down back and adjust.

c ⌐ Arms are supported by chest.

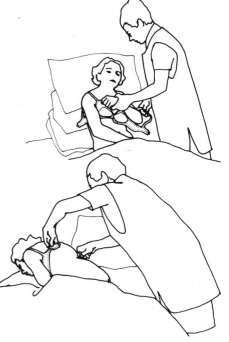

Back opening garment

ʰ ⌐

a Weaker arm threaded in first.

b Second arm threaded in.

⌐ Roll over and fasten.

ʰ Bend forward and fasten.

c If more than one back-opening garment is being put on, roll person over or bend forward and fasten when all garments are on.

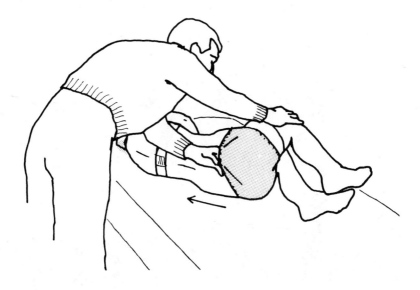

a   Ensure the head is well supported.

b   Roll person away from helper.
    Pull up side of garment.
    Roll towards helper. Pull up other side of garment.

c   Where one knee is stiff, use it as a lever to swing the body over.
    Rolling may be made easier if the leg which is to go underneath is straight
    and the leg to appear on top is bent at the knee.

Lower half garments – brought over feet

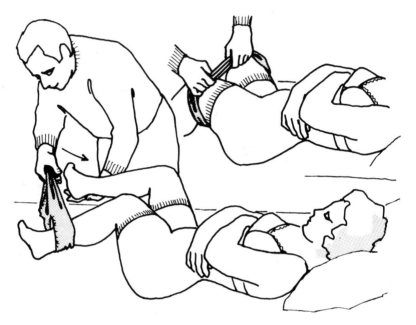

Long skirt/trousers.

a Hands placed comfortably.

b Helper threads one hand through garment leg (or skirt), grasps the appropriate foot and brings it through garment.
Repeat with other leg.
Draw up garment over legs and over knees.
Roll from side to side to pull up garment, or pull up garment when moving from bed to chair.
Fasten.

c Trousers and pants can be brought up as far as knees and then pulled up together.
If desirable, knees can be exercised during dressing.
A zip in inner leg seam may make trousers easier to put on.

d Contra-indicated for tightly bent knees, where a skirt or open flat trousers may be easier.

Lower half garments — over helper's knee or helper seated behind.

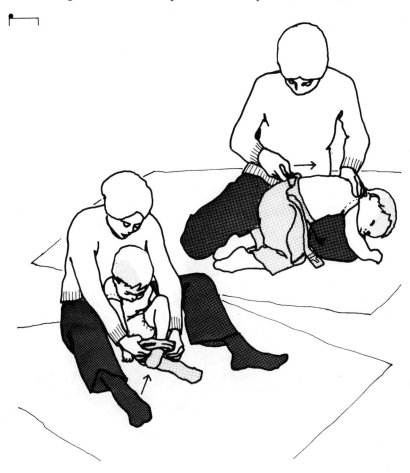

a   Roll down tights or trousers as far as foot.

b   Place child's foot in garment.
    Encourage child to stretch his leg into tights. Place own hands over child's
    hands and draw them up.
    Bend child over knee to bring garment over hips.
    Sit up to fasten.

c   This method is most easily used when seated behind child and so takes
    place on floor.

    Dressing a person from behind can encourage him to help himself.

Hosiery — foot into garment

Helper   A Behind   B in front

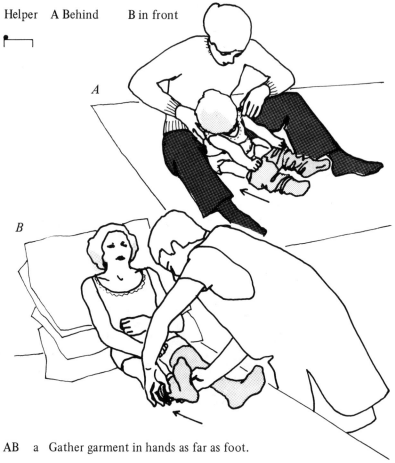

AB a Gather garment in hands as far as foot.

A b Complete as on p. 127.

B b Complete with suspenders. If person is in wheelchair all day, only front suspender may be necessary.

AB c The foot of the garment may be turned back on itself (p. 94 iii).

Socks without heels are easy to put on.
Socks/stockings should not be tight around toes as they may produce/increase deformity.
Suspenders and suspender belt may be replaced by tights/stay-up stockings/socks.

Shoes/Boots

Using ⬯ as aid.

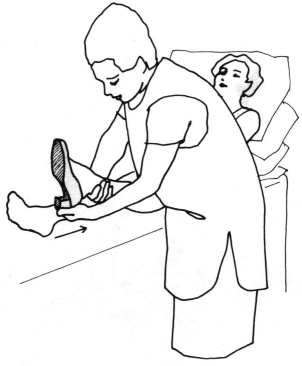

a Undo fastenings.

b Foot should be supported at ankle by one hand, other pulls on shoe/boot.
   Replace foot on bed or stool to fasten.

c Feet for which surgical boots have been prescribed should be put into
   boot with great care to ensure the foot is properly placed inside.
   During an acute attack of arthritis, the ankle should not be moved beyond
   an angle of 90°.
   It may not be necessary for those who are not going to walk to have
   surgical shoes.
   Slipper-socks keep the feet warm for those who are unable to walk and
   whose deformity is too great for ordinary shoes.

Corsetry — open front or side.

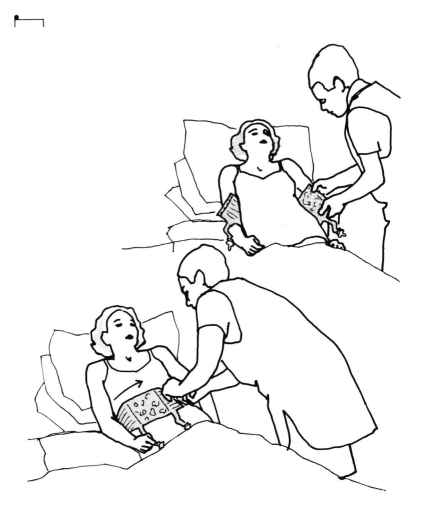

a   Roll to place garment under hips.

b   Roll back, pull garment straight.
Fasten, starting at the bottom.

c   Where a corset is not essential, a small suspender belt which can be pushed
under back or stay-up stockings are alternatives. An elastic, open-flat belt
fastened with Velcro is available. Remove the back suspender or bring it to
the side if the wearer is seated all day.

Long garments with open or half-open back

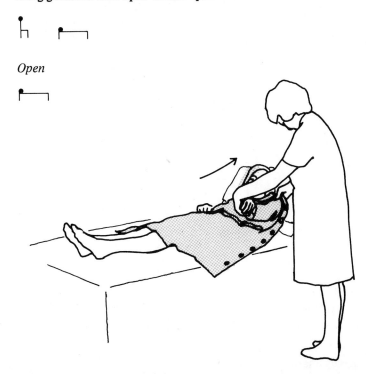

Open

a Open fastenings.
   Place garment over person.

b Lean over and thread first arm through sleeve.
   Tuck garment well under person on same side.
   Repeat for second arm.
   Roll away from helper.
   Pull down and straighten.
   Fasten.

Half-open

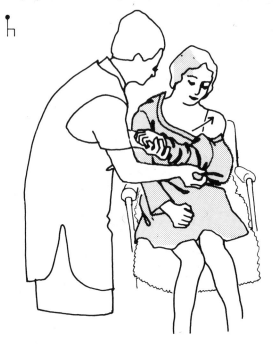

a   Open fastenings.
Stand beside person, gather up dress in hands with back of garment towards the back of patient.

b   Put over head.
Bring down to waist.
Thread first arm through sleeve, supporting at wrist.
Thread second arm through.
Bring garment up on to shoulders.
Lean forward to fasten back.
Roll to pull down or stand to allow skirt to fall.

c   A half-open garment can also be drawn over feet and brought up to hips, then brought up over hips by rolling.

–   A garment opened from the waist to the back hem enables the skirt to be arranged around hips without the person having to be moved.

132

Half-open front

Loose or raglan sleeves.

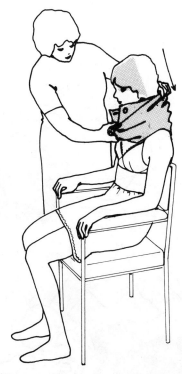

a Open garment.
   Gather garment into circle and put over head.

b Take it down to waist level. (see p. 106).
   Put both arms to back.
   Place hands and arms into sleeves.
   Bring garment up to shoulders.
   Adjust and fasten.

c A split back seam fastened with Velcro, or full back gives more room.
   Open underarm and side seams may be helpful for those with tightly bent
   elbows.

d Contra-indicated for those with tightly bent elbows, painful shoulders.

Additional Garments

Napkin — a sitting method which prevents the child falling back.

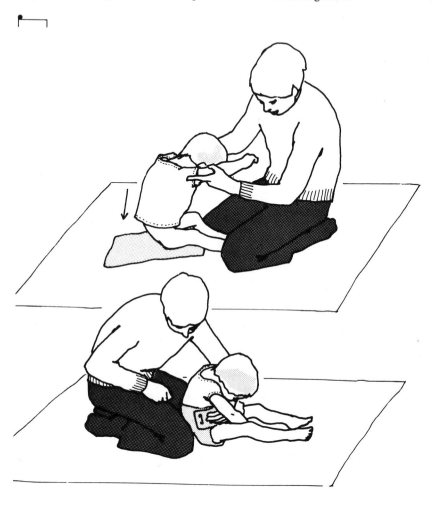

a Hold child under arms and lift.

b Lower him on to napkin, holding him between helper's knees.
Turn him round or move behind him.
Fold napkin round body and fasten.

c Other methods are shown in M. Cornwell's *Early years* pp. 78-81.

CHAPTER 7

TOILETING AND INCONTINENCE

Toileting

Controlling garments in the lavatory causes difficulty to many as it involves partial undressing and dressing as well as control of the garments involved.

All toileting activities, including the removal of clothes where this is necessary, should take place in private. Some people who have become accustomed to institutional life may not seem to have a need for or sense of privacy, but this courtesy should be extended to all.

Micturition and defaecation, the two major excretory functions of the body, normally take place on the lavatory or similar substitute. Males normally micturate standing up, but can use a hand-held urinal while sitting: defaecation and female micturition are normally carried out in a sitting position.

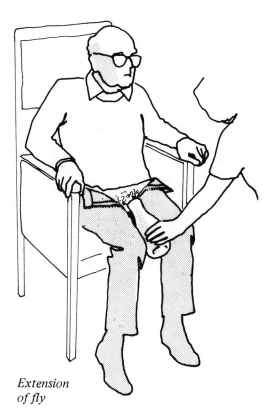

Extension of fly

Standing up to micturate involves standing balance and the need for one free hand to cope with the fly fastenings of underpants and trousers (waistband fasteners are not usually undone). Thus a one-handed person will require good balance, while someone with poor balance will require both hands, using the second hand to hold on to a rail.

Using a hand-held urinal in a chair requires the use of one able hand in order to cope with fly fastenings and to position the urinal correctly. With the usual trouser fly, the urinal has to be removed with an upward movement, so that where there is poor sensation, grip or co-ordination, the urinal may tend to spill as it is removed. Extension of the fly to the crotch helps to overcome this. Where the trouser fly is fastened with a zip, a longer one will be needed; if with Velcro or buttons, the extended opening may appear to be closed without extra fastening. The fly of pyjama trousers may also need to be extended.

Sitting on and using the WC involves the movement of some garments. The activity implies balance, hip mobility, one or both hands with grip and grasp, and adequate length of arm.

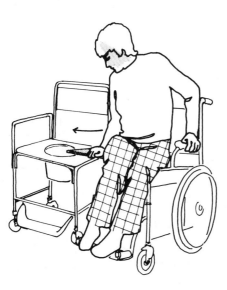

i   Lack of balance can be overcome by using a handrail or other furniture, or by transferring from a chair. Where a disabled person transfers from a chair to the lavatory unaided, it is probably easier to remove clothing after transfer. Garments are pushed down by rolling from side to side or lifting the body on one arm, but should only be pushed as far as is hygienically necessary and not beyond the area of weight bearing, as they are then easier to grasp and pull when sliding forward to return to the chair. A board can be most useful for transfer between chair and lavatory seat, it should be well polished and smooth, and practice both with and without clothing should be tried when it is first used. Sliding forwards or backwards from a wheelchair on to the lavatory may be possible where the chair and seat are on a level and handrails are available.

ii People with stiff hips will find sitting on and rising from the WC easier if the seat is raised or if rails are provided at the side.

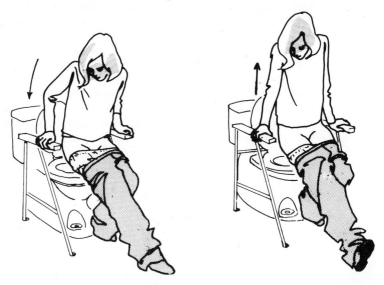

iii Weak hands have diminished grip and grasp (p. 22) but the effect can be countered by various techniques, aids and adaptations. Clothes can be held by the teeth or under the chin;

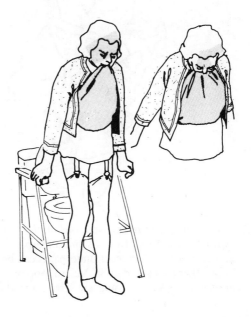

pushed aside by using the hand as a hook; or kept out of the way by being tucked into the waistband, a circle of elastic or belt. Some paralysed arms can be placed to anchor garments keeping one garment in place while the able hand copes with the next garment. Zips in trousers can be inverted and a dressing aid used to open and close them as it is often easier and therefore quicker to pull the zip upwards with an aid. (A further opening has to be provided on the waistband, or the waistband can be elasticated provided the trousers do not fit too closely.) A dressing stick with a cleft at one end can push down pants or knickers and pull them up afterwards. Petticoats can be replaced by lining skirts or dresses to reduce the number of garments to be removed. Braces are helpful if trousers are difficult to manage, as they can be retained by hooking them over the arms when the trousers are unfastened and lowered, and they do not need tight waistband fastenings or belts.

Long underpants usually have loops on the waistband which can be linked up with braces so that trousers and underpants are let down and pulled up together. Loose-fitting short underpants can be used in the same way by sewing either loops or dabs of Velcro loop on to the waistband (corresponding Velcro hooks are sewn on to the trousers). Before standing up, pants and/or trousers should be brought up the thighs as high as possible. Pants and trousers with firm elastic at the waist will remain at mid-thigh level if the knees are kept slightly apart.

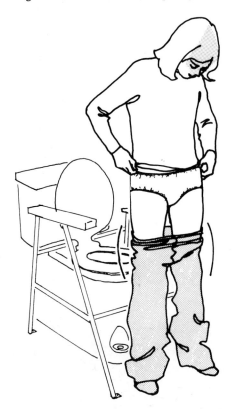

Loose fitting garments are easier than tight fitting ones to pull up and down. Tights are a close fitting garment which may become too difficult to use, but open crotch tights worn with similar pants may be possible and attendants may find them helpful to avoid pulling garments up and down. Stocking tights may be of value to some people.

iv People with a variety of disabilities as well as those with short arms can use a dressing stick to supplement the lack of length. Should garments fall to the floor, a pick-up stick will be needed. A dressing stick can be used to bring the hem of a skirt or shirt to hand level. Braces or long loops which are kept over the arms will keep trousers from falling.
Those without arms or without useful arm activity but with good foot movement can have various adaptations made to clothes to help with independent toileting: the feet can be trained to replace the hands.

Physiotherapists in various units throughout the country will be able to give advice on this.

For a variety of reasons, some people will be dependent upon another for their toileting needs in the lavatory. They can be helped in one of three ways, standing, seated in a chair or wheelchair, or placed in a hoist.

Those with some power in their legs can be encouraged to stand, leaning against a handrail or a wall while the relevant garments are removed; they can then be guided on to the lavatory. It is much easier where the wall or

rail is within easy reach of the lavatory as few foot movements are then involved. Rails beside the lavatory are helpful to take the weight of the disabled person. When someone is seated in a wheelchair, all possible garments should be moved away before transfer to the lavatory takes place. A wrap-round skirt can be left in the chair. Afterwards the trousers and/or pants should be brought up at least as far as the lavatory seat and can be replaced during transfer to the chair where dressing is completed. Garments should be easy to unfasten and remove.

When using a hoist, garments should be adjusted before the slings are put in position. This can be done either on the bed or in a chair. The person is then moved and placed on to the lavatory seat and the lower sling is moved away.

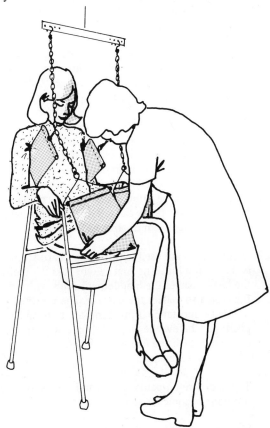

Once he is ready, the lower sling is replaced and he is moved back for redressing. A divided sling means there is no need to remove the lower sling and it should therefore be easier and more comfortable to use.

Urgency of micturition is a problem for some people and can be helped by — the minimum of fastenings: clothes such as an open-back skirt (with open crotch pants), elastic waisted trousers or skirts;

the minimum of garments, including stay-up stockings, suspender tights, or long socks under a long skirt, and not wearing pants; replacing petticoats by lined garments; and taking off two garments together; loose rather than tight garments;

the close proximity and sufficiency of lavatory accommodation, and a regular toileting programme.

Appliances

Some people have to cope with a catheter or a condom with urinal bags; others with an ostomy bag.

i Catheters or condoms and urinal bags are now worn by an increasing number of people, for instance those with a spinal lesion and a paralysed bladder, some of those who are congenitally handicapped or handicapped at birth, and by some incontinent elderly people during retraining programmes. Appliances may leak, if only slightly, so that some padding may be required to absorb it. Leakage is greater if the catheter is kinked so that it is important to ensure that the catheter is free and correctly placed. The urinal bag should be strapped on to the leg in such a way that the catheter is not stretched and the bag is not creating a pressure sore. The bag can be hidden by trousers or a long skirt. To empty the bag, a skirt can be lifted easily, the legs of flare or stretch trousers can be pushed up as far as the tap of the urinal bag, while a zip will be required in the inner leg seam of straight trousers.

ii Ostomy bags are used with three sorts of stoma — colostomy, ileostomy and ileal conduit. The first two bypass the rectum and deal with faeces; the last bypasses the bladder and deals with urine. A bag is attached to the stoma to collect the excreta. The position and length of the stoma is of great importance if problems are to be avoided or minimised. The best position is below the waist and on a smooth area of skin as this makes it easier to attach the bag or dressings; a crease in the skin may cause kinking and therefore leakage.

Tights or stretch pants are useful in preventing the bag from slipping should it become detached.

If supportive corsets are worn they should be made so that the supports avoid the stoma; some elderly people may be able to have a "window" made in the corset with zips down the sides of the window which enable the bag to be emptied. Where a colostomy dressing is preferred, this will also allow it to be adjusted and changed. Clothing should be easily removable so that a bag can be emptied quickly; changing is most easily done in the bath. Those people who have an ileal conduit may have greater problems because the positioning of the stoma may be difficult, and so leakage may occur. They may also have to wear a heavy surgical belt, in which case the bag should be worn outside the belt, brought through a hole made in the belt exactly over the stoma.

The tap of the bag should be angled towards the side for greater comfort if the person is short bodied. Independence in changing bags should be encouraged. For those who have other disabilities, it may be difficult to place bags correctly; dressings can replace colostomy bags but ileostomy and ileal conduit bags are more of a problem, and help from another person may be required.

Toileting area

Briefly, the toileting area should be warm, have facilities for washing hands, and have an accessible surface near at hand. (It may also be needed for changing an ostomy bag). There should be enough room for equipment such as wheelchairs and hoists and for a helper to move easily. Handrails provide stability for people who have poor balance, are one-handed, have weak knees or hips, or poor co-ordination. Handrails should be positioned at the right height and angle to withstand the pressure exerted when the person sits down or stands up, and guidance about rails should be sought from therapists employed by the local authority or the health authority, or, in a domestic situation, from the disabled person himself.

The lavatory should be at a comfortable height; it is sometimes easier if the cover of the lavatory seat is removed; the seat itself should be easy to raise and well supported at the back, and should be solid enough to withstand the full weight of the person using it if he has to drop down on to it, for example someone with stiff hips or stiff knees. (Some types of plastics, when cold, are liable to fracture on impact.) In this latter case, a raised seat may be useful.

The flush should be accessible and easy to operate. Some lavatory bowls incorporate a washing and drying mechanism so that transfer from lavatory to bidet or the use of toilet paper is avoided. Water and air should be pre-set at the correct temperature. Sani-chairs can be used to wheel someone over the lavatory bowl, enabling undressing and transfer on to the chair to take place outside the room, if space is limited.

Commodes and chemical closets are useful where there are not enough toilet facilities, or they are too far away for the person to reach.

Incontinence

This is a problem for people of all ages and with many disabilities. It can be the cause of great unhappiness, breakdown of family relationships, admission to an institution or, in some cases, refusal of institutional care.

The young child is not expected to have control over his bladder or bowel until he reaches an age when he can understand what is wanted of him and his mother can train him in socially acceptable habits. If training is not appropriate, for whatever reason, the problem of coping with wet and soiled napkins and clothes gradually increases as the child himself grows larger and heavier.

Once continence has been achieved, any return to the incontinent state is not only socially unacceptable but also a shock to the sufferer which must be taken into account. Incontinence is not a condition that should be automatically accepted and protective pads and pants provided. Prevention of the condition, and ways of returning to continence, are both most important. A positive approach will help both sufferer and helper.

i   Aids to prevention of incontinence:

Easy access to warm toilet facilities and the right height of bed, wheelchair or commode for easy transfer from one piece of furniture to another.

Regular visits to the toilet.

Clothes which allow quick undressing.

General mental stimulus through activities and interests.

Good environment, including carpets on the floor, comfortable attractive seating and clean bright decoration, and clothing which is individual to each person.

ii Aids to return to continence:

Investigation of any medical reason for incontinence, and treatment instituted where possible.

Charting the time incontinence occurs and basing visits to the toilet on this.

Clothes which allow quick undressing.

Easy access to toilet areas, as in (i).

iii Clothing for quick undressing:

Open back skirts and petticoats.

Open crotch pants or loose pants which are easy to push down (French knickers, silky non-static fabric).

Elastic waisted trousers with underpants attached.

Trouser zip replaced by Velcro.

Drop-front or drop-back trousers with pants to match.

Extended fly front opening.

iv	Clothing for constantly incontinent people:	Separates for women, the skirt open back, with open back waist petticoats if a petticoat is essential.
		Bodices or a narrow suspender belt for stockings if corsets are not required.
		Stockings or suspender tights are more suitable than tights.
		Open back nightdresses, nightshirts, dressing gowns.
		"Shortie" nightdresses worn with pants (only the pants have to be changed).
		Elastic waisted trousers (also pyjama trousers).
		Shirts with tails shortened or sports shirts and sweaters.
		Washable shoes and slippers.
v	Fabrics etc:	Easily washable, durable, shrink resistant, able if necessary to withstand boiling and always to look presentable.
		Fastenings able to withstand constant wear and firmly sewn on.

vi Protective garments and pads help to protect the clothing, but the incontinent person should continue to be changed as soon as micturition has taken place as few of the pads supplied by manufacturers can absorb the amount of urine normally voided by an adult or older child. Excess urine will therefore tend to leak out and damp the clothes outside. If the pad can be made from a length of padding roll the thickness can be adjusted. Protective garments should be well-fitting.

Geriatric chairs with tables in front and cot sides on beds can be deterrents to continence as the occupier may feel trapped and unable to move. Cot sides should be removed as soon as possible as they can encourage someone already confused to think he has returned to infancy, and thus to incontinence.

Where possible wet or soiled garments should not be brought over the head of an incontinent person.

A great deal of time and patience can be spent in changing clothing so that a study of the ways in which the type of clothing impedes or quickens the process may be worthwhile. For instance, tight trousers take longer to remove when wet; an open-flat protective garment will allow for the removal of an inner pad with the minimum of disturbance of other clothes where the person is lying flat.

Clothing Adaptations and Fastenings

Adaptations to garments and different garments and fastenings can help in the management of toileting and of incontinence (see also Macartney, P. *Clothes sense).*

i *Adaptations*

Trousers:	Extended fly.
	Drop front) to avoid pulling garments up Drop back) and down.
	Zip reversed for easier unfastening (p. 138).
	Overlap of the fly extended to avoid the front fly fastenings.

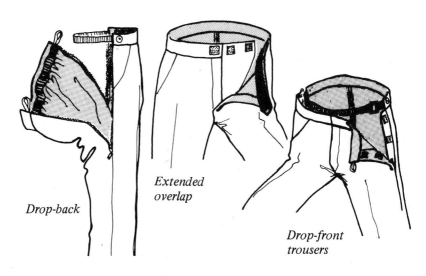

Drop-back

Extended overlap

Drop-front trousers

Skirts, dresses, nightdresses and petticoats:	Open back — skirt can be drawn to the side rather than pulled up. Also obviates need to pull wet garment over the head.
	Floating panel — covers open back seam.
Pants (male):	Drop back or front to match trousers.
	Open flat.
	Extended fly to cover open flat incontinence garment.
	Sailor flaps.

Pants (female):	Lengthened gusset to avoid pulling garment up and down.

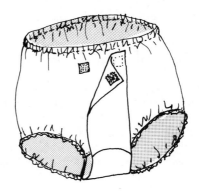

	Gusset removed (to make an open crotch style).
	Open flat.
Shirts:	Shirt tails removed to prevent them getting wet.
ii *Different Garments*	Loose garments are easier to put on and take off.
Pants (female):	Open crotch, French knickers.
Pants (male):	Boxer shorts.
Petticoats:	Waist style, for the incontinent.
Skirts:	Wrap over. Open back. Floating panel.
Tights:	Open crotch or stocking tights.
Trousers:	Elastic waistband.
Top clothing:	Separates for women (skirts are more easily replaceable in case of accidents).
Shirts:	T-shirts or sports shirts.
iii *Different fastenings:*	Fastenings that are easier to undo (see Chapter 5).

Toileting is not a simple area of dressing, but it does entail much that is essential for the comfort and wellbeing of all. Time which is spent on discussing the various aspects of toileting and how they can be made easier will be time well spent.

CHAPTER 8

SOME CONCLUSIONS

1 This book has not been an easy one to write, as there are many more facets to dressing and dressing skills than at first appear. It was therefore thought useful to pick up some of the thoughts to be found throughout the text and to bring them together at the end as a guide.

2 Dressing is a skill which takes time and perseverance to learn, which may be compounded when there is a disability. There are infinite variations on the theme, for no one person dresses exactly as another and everyone reacts differently to each disability. The helper can make suggestions from her experience or the therapist give guidance from her knowledge but each disabled person has to find out for himself the best way to dress and the easiest clothes to put on.

3 There are few people who are so helpless that they can do nothing for themselves — they can choose clothes they like, push an arm into a sleeve or adjust a seam, and they should be encouraged to do all they can.

4 Ingenuity, imagination and experimentation by all who are involved can help to produce or restore independent dressing.

5 Therapists have much advice and knowledge to give in the field of dressing and, in the interests of those to whom they give care, both therapists and helpers should ensure that a planned programme of rehabilitation of dressing skills is carried through. Helpers could also be trained to assess progress and to ask for further help when it is required.

6 Research can be used in several ways: on the use of time (p. 15); methods of communication between helper, therapist, the person being helped and relatives (p. 24); improvement and increase of knowledge of clothing so that the most suitable garments combined with the best methods of dressing, can be offered to disabled people (p. 26); and on the best garments and methods for easy changing of incontinent people (p. 145).

7 Dressing should be seen as a necessary part of living and therefore of rehabilitation. Such an emphasis may also help the disabled person himself to look at dressing and clothing in a more positive light, able to discard or adopt alternative methods or garments more easily.

8 It has not proved possible within the confines of this book to include very much about the choice of garments, or how to modify or alter them, and yet this could be seen to be an essential part of dressing. Two Disabled

Living Foundation booklets — G. Forbes' *Clothing for the handicapped child* and P. Macartney's *Clothes sense* which give help and advice in this area are therefore recommended.

9 The methods of dressing described in the book have not been related to any particular disability as people react to the same degree of the same disability in very different ways. However, some voluntary organisations for specific disabilities have produced pamphlets about dressing including the Royal National Institute for the Blind and the Friends of the Centre for Spastic Children (App III) which give some very helpful hints.

APPENDIX I

STATUTORY BODIES

Local education department: Parents of children needing clothing and footwear (including school uniform and sports clothing) may qualify for school uniform and clothing grants if they have insufficient money. The benefit is means tested and applicants should get a claim form from the local education office.

The Department of Health and Social Security: People of 16 and over may qualify for supplementary benefits. The supplementary benefits scale rates are intended to provide for normal living expenses, including the replacement of clothing and footwear. However, an extra discretionary allowance may be made to someone whose footwear or clothing is subjected to heavy wear and tear, or who needs to purchase special items of clothing, due to mental or physical illness, disability or handicap. This does not include items that need to be replaced in the normal course of events eg. because they are outgrown or outworn.

Single lump sum payments may be made to those qualifying for supplementary benefits in cases of exceptional need. If you have more than £300 in savings, a single payment will be reduced by the amount your savings exceed £300. Full details regarding these payments are available from Social Security Offices.

A wide range of body-worn surgical appliances is available through the National Health Service hospitals on the recommendation of a hospital consultant. Most appliances are individually made to suit the needs of patients and include surgical footwear, elastic hosiery, breast prostheses and bras and wigs. A charge is made for wigs, fabric support garments and elastic hosiery supplied to hospital out-patients. Some people may be exempt from this charge and help is also available on income grounds. Some garments for people who are incontinent may be supplied through the Health Services as well as Social Services eg. protective underwear. In hospitals, other items of clothing are provided according to need. *Help for Handicapped People,* available free from any Social Security Office has helpful information.

Voluntary bodies

Women's Royal Voluntary Service: In many parts of the country, the WRVS has clothing stores to which people can be referred by doctors, health visitors, district nursing sisters, social workers and others. Each store is administered differently, but evidence of need must normally be produced. WRVS sewing groups will often help with adaptations to garments.

Charities: There are a number of charities which may be able to help those in

150

exceptional need, including the organisations for specific disabilities, Forces benevolent societies, trade unions, the Lady Hoare Trust and the Marie Curie Memorial Foundation (see App. III). Help is normally considered only when the person falls within the group of people helped by that particular charity and where other help has been exhausted. Children, under 16, who are severely handicapped may receive help from the Family Fund (see App. III).

APPENDIX II

BIBLIOGRAPHY

a Books

Agras, W.S. *Behaviour modification,* 2nd ed. Boston, Little & Brown, 1978.

Baldwin, V.L. et al. *Isn't it time he outgrew this?–a training programme for parents of retarded children.* Springfield, Ill. Charles C. Thomas, 1976.

Bowley, A. and Gardiner, L. *The handicapped child,* 4th ed. Edinburgh, Churchill Livingstone, 1980.

Bumphrey, E.E. and Stevens, B.M. *Dressmaking for the disabled,* rev. ed. 1981. Assistant Editor, British Journal of Occupational Therapy, 20 Rede Place, London W2 4TU.

Carr, J. and Wilson, B. Self-help skills. *In* Yule, W. and Carr, J. eds. *Behaviour modification for the mentally handicapped.* London, Croom Helm, 1980.

Cornwell, M. *Early years.* London, Disabled Living Foundation, 1975.

Disabled Living Foundation. Information Lists: *Clothing,* No. 13; *Footwear,* No. 14, from the Information service, DLF (annually updated).

England, M.D. *Footwear for problem feet.* London, Disabled Living Foundation, 1973.

Equipment for the Disabled. *Clothing and dressing for adults,* 5th ed. 1981, *Disabled child,* 4th ed. 1980. Brighton, Equipment for the Disabled.

Finnie, N. *Handling the young cerebral palsied child at home,* rev. ed. London, Heinemann Medical Books, 1975.

Forbes, G. *Clothing for the handicapped child.* London, Disabled Living Foundation, 1971.

Gibson, J. and French, T. *Nursing the mentally retarded.* 4th ed. London, Faber & Faber, 1978.

Goldsworthy, M. *Clothes for disabled people,* Oxford, Batsford, 1981.

Grant, W.R. *Principles of rehabilitation.* Edinburgh, E. & S. Livingston, 1963.

Harris, A.I. *Handicapped and impaired in Great Britain.* London, HMSO, 1971.

Hodkinson, M. *Nursing the elderly.* Oxford, Pergamon, 1967.

Hoffman, A.M. *Clothing for the handicapped, the aged and other people with special needs.* Springfield, Ill., Charles C. Thomas, 1979.

Hollingworth S. *Knitting and crochet for the physically handicapped and elderly.* London, Batsford, 1981.

Jay, P. *Help yourselves: a handbook for hemiplegics and their families,* 3rd ed. Hornchurch, Ian Henry, 1979.

Johnson, D.F. *Total patient care.* St. Louis, C.V. Mosby, 1972.

Kings Fund Centre. *Report of a study conference on headgear for epileptics, December 1973.* London, Kings Fund Centre.

Kings Fund Centre. *Report of a study conference on fabrics and clothing in hospitals, December 1971.* Papers by Mrs J. Lord, Mr R. Stubbs, Mr O. Grant. London, Kings Fund Centre.

Lord, J. *Clothing for the handicapped and disabled: a bibliography 1937-1970.* Manchester, Shirley Institute, 1970.

Macartney, P. *Clothes sense for handicapped adults of all ages.* London, Disabled Living Foundation, 1973.

MacDonald, E.M. ed. *Occupational therapy in rehabilitation,* 4th ed. London, Macmillan, 1976.

Mandelstam, D. *Incontinence.* London, Heinemann Health Books, 1977.

Mandelstam, D. ed. *Incontinence and its management.* London, Croom Helm, 1980.

Nichols, P. *Living with a handicap.* London, Priory Press, 1973 (out of print).

Norton D. *An investigation of geriatric nursing problems in hospital.* London, National Corporation for the Care of Old People, 1962.

Westridge, L. *Techniques for daily living and guides.* Jacksonville, Illinois School for Visually Impaired, 1970.

Wilks, J. and E. *Bernard—bringing up our mongol son.* London, Routledge and Keegan Paul, 1974.

Willborger, P. and Bresman, G. *Perceptual motor dysfunction.* Seminar report 1965. USA.

b Journal, articles

Brocklehurst, J.C. Incontinence in the elderly. *Nursing Mirror,* Sutton, Surrey 1973. vol. 136, no. 1 pp. 30-32.

Hallenbeck, P.N. and Behrens, D.A. Clothing problems of the retarded. *Mental Retardation,* Washington 1967, vol. 5, pp. 21-24.

Heddle, S. Clothing hints for people in wheelchairs. *MSS Bulletin.* London, 1980, no. 67, pp. 873-874.

Karen, R.L. and Maxwell, S.J. Strengthening self-help behaviour in the retarded. *American Journal of Mental Deficiency,* New York, 1967, vol. 71, pp. 545-550.

Martin, G.L. et al. Operant conditioning in dressing behavior of severely retarded girls. *Mental Retardation,* Columbus, 1971, vol. 9, pp. 27-31.

Moore, P. and Carr, J. A behaviour modification programme to teach dressing to a severely retarded adolescent. *Nursing Times,* London, September 1976.

Renbourn, E.T. Clothes make the man. The psychology of dress. *Ciba-Geigy Review,* Basel, 1964-5.

Royal National Institute for the Blind. Making life easier. *New Beacon,* London, 1969, vol. 8, no. 623 pp. 59-65.

Rudd, T.N. The background to rehabilitation: clothes rehabilitation. *Nursing Mirror,* Sutton, Surrey, 16 July, 1965, pp. 373-374.

Textile care labelling—revised code aims to help the consumer. *BSI News,* London, 1980, February, pp. 10-11.

Thornton, M. Changing gear: adaptation of patients' own trousers. *New Age,* Mitcham, 1979, vol. 6, p. 32.

Thornton, M. Clothing for the handicapped. *Midwife, Health Visitor and Community Nurse,* London, 1980, vol. 16, no. 2, pp. 67-70.

Thornton, M. Clothing for the handicapped, the elderly, the incontinent and the infirm. *Handicaps Monthly,* Singapore, 1979, December, pp. 75, 77 and 79.

Turnbull, E.M. A male stroke's dressing problems. *British Journal of Occupational Therapy,* London, 1977, vol. 40, pp. 248-249.

Wilson, D. Clever clothing for the handicapped. *Journal of Community Nursing,* Sutton, Surrey, 1980, vol. 4, no. 3, pp. 28-29.

APPENDIX III

USEFUL ADDRESSES

Age Concern
60 Pitcairn Road
Mitcham Surrey
01-640 5431

Arthritis Care
6 Grosvenor Crescent
London SW1X 7ER
01-235 0902

Association to Combat Huntington's Chorea
Borough House
34A Station Road
Hinckley
Leics. LE10 1AP
0455-615558

Association for Research into Restricted Growth
Chairman:
4 Laburnum Avenue
Wickford, Essex
03744 3132

Association for Spina Bifida and Hydrocephalus
Tavistock House North
Tavistock Square
London WC1H 9HJ
01-388 1382

British Epilepsy Association
Crowthorne House
New Wokingham Road
Wokingham
Berkshire RG11 3AY
034 46 3122

British Limbless Ex-Servicemen's Association
Frankland Moore House
185-187 High Road
Chadwell Heath
Essex RM6 6NA
01-590 1124

British Polio Fellowship
Bell Close
West End Road
Ruislip, Middlesex
71 75515

British Red Cross Society
9 Grosvenor Crescent
London SW1
01-235 5454

Brittle Bone Society
112 City Road
DD2 2PW
0382 67603

Chest Heart and Stroke Association
Tavistock House North
Tavistock Square
London WC1H 9HJ
01-387 3012

Colostomy Welfare Group
38/39 Eccleston Square
London SW1
01-828 5175

Disabled Drivers Association
Ashwellthorpe
Norwich, Norfolk
NR16 1EX
050 841 449

Disablement Income Group (DIG)
Attlee House
28 Commercial Street
London E1 6LR
01-247 2128/6877

Downs Children's Association
Quinborne Centre
Ridgacre Road
Quinton, Birmingham B32 2TW
021 427 1374

Family Fund
Beverley House
Shipton Road
York YO3 6RB
0904 21115

Friends of the Centre for Spastic Children
63 Cheyne Walk
London SW3 5NA
01-352 6740

Haemophilia Society
PO Box 9
16 Trinity Street
London SE1 1DE
01-407 1010

Help the Aged
32 Dover Street
London W1A 2AP
01-499 0972

Ileostomy Association of Great Britain and Northern Ireland
Central Office
Amblehurst House
Chobham
Woking, Surrey GU24 8PZ
09905 8277

Invalids at Home
17 Lapstone Gardens
Kenton
Harrow HA3 0BB
01-907 1706

Marie Curie Memorial Foundation
138 Sloane Square
London SW1
01-730 9157

Mastectomy Association
1 Colworth Road
Croydon
Surrey CR0 7AD
01-654 8643

Multiple Sclerosis Society of Great Britain and Northern Ireland
286 Munster Road
Fulham, London SW6 6AP
01-381 4022-5

Muscular Dystrophy Group of Great Britain and Northern Ireland
Nattras House
35 Macauley Road
London SW4 0QP
01-720 8055

National Association for Mental Health
22 Harley Street
London W1N 2ED
01-637 0741

National Eczema Society
Tavistock House North
Tavistock Square
London WC1H 9HJ
01-388 4097

National Elfrida Rathbone Society
11a Whitworth Street
Manchester M1 3GW
061 236 5358

National Fund for Research into Crippling Diseases
(Action for the Crippled Child)
Vincent House
Springfield Road
Horsham
Sussex
0403 64101

Parkinson's Disease Society
81 Queens Road
London SW19
01-946 2500

Royal Association for Disability and Rehabilitation
25 Mortimer Street
London W1N 8AB
01-637 5400

Royal National Institute for the Deaf
105 Gower Street
London WC1 E6AH
01-387 8033

Royal Society for Mentally Handicapped Children and Adults
117 Golden Lane
London EC1Y 0RT
01-253 9433

Scottish Council for Spastics
22 Corstorphine Road
Edinburgh EH126 HP
031 337 9876

Scottish Council on Disability
18/19 Claremont Crescent
Edinburgh EH1 6HP
031 556 3882

Scottish Epilepsy Association
48 Govan Road
Glasgow GS1 1JL
041 427 4911

Spastics Society
12 Park Crescent
London W1N 4EQ
01-636 5020

Spinal Inuries Association
5 Crowndale Road
London NW1 1TV
01-388 6840

Thistle Foundation
Headquarters:
27A Walker Street
Edinburgh EH3 7HX
031 225 7282

Women's Royal Voluntary Service
17 Old Park Lane
London W1Y 4AJ
01-499 6040

INDEX

Index for Illustrations of dressing methods